In the name of Allah, Most Beneficent, Most Merciful
CAREGIVING TO MUSLIMS
A GUIDE FOR CHAPLAINS, COUNSELORS, HEALTHCARE AND SOCIAL WORKERS

Imam Muhammad Hatim PhD, DMin
With A Foreword By
Rev. Willard W.C. Ashley, Sr. DMin, DH

Caregiving to Muslims: A Guide for Chaplains, Counselors, Healthcare and Social Workers

Copyright © 2017 by Muhammad Hatim

All rights reserved. No part of this book may be reproduced or transmitted in any form or by any means, electronic or mechanical, including photocopying, recording, scanning, or by any information storage and retrieval system without written permission from the Muhammad Hatim.

Cover photo: Muhammad Hatim, Al-Aqsa Masjid, Jerusalem

ISBN-13: 978-1542401081
ISBN-10: 1542401089

Printed in the United States of America

DEDICATION

This book is dedicated to the people who have most influenced my formative years. I thank them for their patience, direction, love, and understanding. These include Dorothy Mae Carson, my recently deceased mother. She gave me the gift of life. She encouraged and inspired me to read and study. Mary Lucille Simms, my grandmother, was the example who showed me the meaning and benefit of righteous behavior. Emery Simms, my grandfather, set the standard for manhood and family dedication. I thank Sylvia Knight-Rose, my sister, for her unconditional love and support. And, I thank Richard Knight, my absented deceased father for being the mysterious canvass upon which my life is drawn. Also, I dedicate this book to descendants of enslaved Muslims forced to immigrate to America as well as Muslim pioneers who courageously reclaimed the religion of Al-Islam in America.

Table of Contents

FOREWORD 9
PROLOGUE 1 11
PROLOGUE 2 14
ACKNOWLEDGEMENTS 18
PREFACE 19
   Why Write This Book? 19
   Presidential Campaign of 2016 and American Muslims 20
   What Have I Observed? 22
   Chapter Roadmap 25
INTRODUCTION 27
Chapter 1: Fundamentals of Al-Islam 31
   What is Al-Islam? 32
   Who are the Muslims? 32
   Islamic Faith and Worship 33
   Islamic Points of Belief 35
   Islamic Worship (Ibadah) System 39
   The Glorious Qur'an 42
   The Importance of Covenants in Al-Islam 44
      Definition of Covenant 44
      Covenant with Prophet Adam (as) 45
      Covenant with Prophet Ibrahim (as) and His Descendants 46
      Covenant with Prophet Ishmael (as) 46
      Covenant with Prophet Muhammad (pbuh) 47

    Responsible Actions Covered by the Divine Covenant 48

    Summary Comments 49

Chapter 2: Basis of Holistic Pastoral Care for Muslims 51

  The Meaning and Purpose of the Human Soul (Nafs) 52

  Selected Spiritual Challenges within the Muslim Community 54

    Introduction 54

    Selected Roles of the Imam 55

    Chaplaincy, Counseling, and Caregiving 59

    Qur'an and Counseling/Helping Relationship 60

    Hermeneutics of Suspicion 62

    Trusting Relationship with Christians and Jew 63

    Cultural Competence 64

    Psychologists and Spiritual Cultural Competency 66

    Human Devils 67

Chapter 3: Al-Islam, Muslims, and American Health Care 70

  Introduction 71

  Psycho-Spiritual Concerns of Contemporary American Muslims. 73

    Historic Qur'anic/Biblical Perspective 73

    Spiritual Roots of Religious Conflict 75

    Selected Muslim Psycho-socio-spiritual Concerns 76

    African American Muslims 77

    Immigrant Muslims 87

    Summary 91

Chapter 4: The Culture/Tradition of the Muslim Family 94

The Family in Al-Islam 95
Examples of Specific Equal Treatment Between Men and Women
.... 98
The Divine Revelation and Rationale Concerning Polygamy 100
Islam and Gay, Lesbian, Bisexual, Transgender and Questioning
(GLBTQ) Believers 102
   Introduction 102
   Islamic Considerations 102
   Secular GLBTQ Considerations 105
   Caregiving and Psychological Considerations 106
   Summary 110

Chapter 5: Identifying the Spiritual Roots of Terrorism 115
   Introduction 116
   Oppression Is Worse Than Death 118
   Qur'anic Right of Self-Defense 122
   Individual Psychology Verses Sociology and Terrorism 122
   Terrorists and Narcissistic Traits 125
   Terrorism and Group Psychology 125
   Reflection 126

Chapter 6: Al-Islam and Clinical Analysis 128
   Caregiving from an Islamic Perspective 129
   Fundamental Spiritual Concerns 132
      Introduction 132
      Creation Story: Adam and His Mate 134
   Comparative Discussions on the Psyche/Soul (Nafs) 136

- Al-Qur'an 136
- Sigmund Freud 137
- Alfred Adler 137
- Viktor Frankl 138
- Fitra 138
- Pastoral Care Models 141
- When Elephants Quarrel, the Grass Suffers 145
- Chapter 7: The Caregiver and Muslim Spiritual Assessment 148
- Pruyser's Diagnostic Variables 149
- Relationship of Pruyser's Variables to Al-Qur'an 150
  - Awareness of the Holy: 150
  - Providence: 152
  - Faith 153
  - Gratefulness 155
  - Repentance 156
  - Communion 157
  - Vocation 159
- Selected Brief Case Studies 160
  - Case 1 162
  - Case 2 164
  - Case 3 165
  - Case 4 168
  - Case 5 170
- APPENDICES 172

A.	Honorifics Used in This Book	172
B.	Transliterated Useful Phrases	172
C.	Selected Arabic Words	173
REFERENCES		175

FOREWORD

I was honored when Dr. Hatim asked me to contribute to his book. *Caregiving to Muslims: A Guide for Chaplains, Counselors, Healthcare and Social Workers* is a major contribution to the caregiving professions. His work will go a long way to assist caregivers to provide culturally competent services to Muslim individuals, as well as the Muslim Community. As a psychotherapist, ordained Baptist Minister, seminary administrator, and teacher, I realize the importance of this work.

I am aware that his book is the result of Imam Hatim's many years of experience in ministering to Muslims and non-Muslims. We have had the opportunity many times to share perspectives and comment on challenges in our respective communities. Dr. Hatim has worked as a chaplain to prisoners and correction officers. He worked with residents and staff at various hospitals and nursing homes. He has years of experience as a substance use disorder/mental health counselor. As an Imam for many years, he is intimately familiar with the vagaries and challenges of providing care to Muslims.

I first came to know Imam Hatim when I worked as the Project Director for the Care for the Caregivers Interfaith Program, Council of Churches of the City of New York. It was the largest clergy resiliency program in the United States. We were a driving force for pastoral care during and immediately after the World Trade Center Disaster of September 11, 2001.

Imam Hatim; Shaykh Abdullah Latif Ali, now deceased leader of the Admiral Family Circle Islamic Community (Admiral Family); Ummi Nur Ali; and Shaykh Dr. Ibrahim Abdul-Malik were intimately involved in the interfaith program. They were also Red Cross Disaster Chaplains. They participated in learning transferable techniques and strategies that could be useful to themselves and to other Muslim leaders during and immediately after the September 11th crisis period. In fact, they subsequently offered culturally competent training to various Muslims communities in the New York City metropolitan area.

Dr. Hatim and Shaykh Dr. Ibrahim continue to offer such training to various Muslim communities. Dr. Hatim was a victim of and actually witnessed the 911 attack five blocks from the twin towers. This book represents the further intellectual and practical development of experiential material in a way that can be meaningful to both Muslim and non-Muslim clinicians and caregivers.

Caregiving to Muslims: A Guide for Chaplains, Counselors, Healthcare and Social Workers presents for the first time, an intimate look into the challenges that some Imams and Muslim caregivers have to face while interacting with Christian-dominated Clinical Pastoral Education (CPE) organizations. Imam Hatim suggested that CPE leadership more often is at the very least ambivalent, if not subliminally hostile, to Muslim and other non-Christian trainees throughout the CPE process. He suggested that CPE become more aware of its *showdown self*. In an innovative way, Dr. Hatim takes an in-depth look at the *Spiritual Roots of Terrorism* as well as what he calls the *Spiritual Roots of Religious Conflict*. As an Imam, Board Certified Clinical Chaplain, Board Certified Pastoral Counselor, and Certified Alcohol and Drug Counselor, he possesses a unique perspective.

As the nation moves to *healing the great divide,* it is incumbent upon clinicians working with Muslims to access the best tools possible. Imam Hatim's book gives suggestions on using applicable strategies and theories that are useful and can help clinicians and caregivers find common ground.

The Reverend Willard Ashley, Sr., DMin., DH
Dean of the Seminary - Associate Professor of Practical Theology
New Brunswick Theological Seminary
Editor, *Learning to Lead: Lessons in Leadership for People of Faith*
Co-editor, *Disaster Spiritual Care, 2nd Edition*

New York, NY
January 2, 2017

PROLOGUE I

> Caregiving is an *art* that allows the patient to paint on his/her human canvass with the vibrant colors of wellness. Clinicians are the compassionate witnesses who encourage these masterpieces.

So writes Dr. Muhammad Hatim in his very useful, thought-provoking book. Perhaps more than any other two sentences throughout the work, the words of the preceding quote capture the spirit and essence of his message. To all who undertake the sacred role of guiding their fellow humans through their healing journey to achieve their higher levels of well-being, he speaks with compassion and conviction.

Dr. Hatim is clear about why he is primarily motivated to help his non-Muslim colleagues become more effective in their clinical interactions with their Muslim clients. He is always respectful of the skills and training of his fellow practitioners; but he insists that for them to be at their professional best with Muslim clients, they must be/become familiar with their life styles and cultural traditions.

Even as he is issuing this seeming edict, Dr. Hatim devotes enough time to explaining why cultural competency is a necessary part of the well-trained clinician's knowledge base. He not only presents his own compelling arguments, but he bolsters those arguments with citations and practical examples from some highly-respected authorities in the field – Sigmund Freud, Alfred Adler, Carl Jung, Carl Rogers, Viktor Frankl.

Muslim Caregivers! Do not assume that because the primary target readers are your non-Muslim colleagues, therefore this book has nothing for you. On the contrary, Dr. Hatim speaks equally to you, particularly when he goes beyond the topic of cultural competency. When, for example, he strongly recommends that counselors and clinicians follow Carl Rogers' five principles: • Be true to yourself, • Permit yourself to understand the other person, • Open channels for authentic communication, • Be accepting of differences/distinctions, •

Allow the patient to tell his/her own story without interference, he is also speaking to YOU.

When, for example, he cites Dr. Frankl's words: *A therapist who ignores man's spiritual side, and is thus forced to ignore the will-to-meaning, is giving away one of his most valuable assets.* **<u>For it is to this will that a psychotherapist should appeal</u>** (emphasis added), he is also speaking to YOU. He is urging YOU, and all clinicians, to include (in his words) some aspect of a *spiritual assessment.*

As Muslim Caregivers, you know, as certainly does Dr. Hatim, that the Muslim Community in the United States is **not** monolithic. Yet he takes the time to remind ALL of his readers not to fall into the too common pattern of acting as if *to know one Muslim is to know all Muslims.*

Under ordinary circumstances, such a reminder would be considered par for the course, because it emphasizes the importance of treating every Muslim client as an individual, irrespective of what may be true or assumed about *Muslims as a group/community*. It is therefore incumbent on each practitioner to do his/her homework.

In response to the events of September 11, 2001, (and to all of the later ones, Muslim-related or imagined), the public attitude towards Muslims in the United States is arguably at its worst ever. Dr. Hatim properly recognizes how this history can affect the judgment of even the most fair-minded among us. He warns:

> America has a *shadow self* (Jung, 1933, pg.35) that informs its relationship with Muslims around the world. This shadow may fall as well on caregivers here in the US. It may influence the individual encounter in subtle ways.

The specifics of this warning clearly are aimed at Dr. Hatim's primary group – non-Muslim counselors and clinicians. But only the least thoughtful reader would miss the equally powerful message that is being sent to their Muslim counterparts. The message?

> Be ever so careful not to allow your silent prejudices and stereotypes to get in the way of your interactions with individuals whom you perceive as representing the group/community which is the object of those prejudices and stereotypes.

How wise of Dr. Hatim! Clearly, he recognizes how easy it is for any of us, the most open-minded, to allow our intellect to convince us that WE have escaped the insidious influences of the very society that has nurtured us, and in which we still live and work.

CAREGIVING TO MUSLIMS-- A Guide For Chaplains, Counselors, Healthcare And Social Workers lives up to its professional promise. It also speaks to the souls of those who seek its counsel.

Shaykh Ibrahim Abdul-Malik, EdD, PhD
Assistant Professor, Fairleigh Dickerson University
Certified Master Practitioner: Neuro-Linguistic Programming (NLP) & Ericksonian Therapeutic Hypnosis, Life Coach –
Nutritionist, Author: Islam and Muslims: Twenty-Five Questions and Answers.

New York City
September 29, 2016

PROLOGUE 2

This work is valuable for several reasons. The most prominent reason is the need to fill a vacuum on resources to address the issues of consciousness, spirituality, and integrated wellness for Muslims. This important work is a major contribution to cultural competency in clinical assessment and analysis. It recognizes what is essentially the significance of Muslim spirit, and the celestial heart. It accomplishes this in a continuum through a necessary conversation that begins in mind, body and spirit matters as seen through an Islamic set of lenses. Also, it offers a necessary discussion and could act as a valuable resource for the professionals who interact with Muslim individuals, families and groups in the *American Public square*. Those domains are inclusive of both public and private sector spaces within this square which seek to offer a holistic view of the human family.

The perspective of indigenous African-American Muslim scholars on the traditional training in clinical pastoral education (CPE), cultural competency, and credentialing is sorely missing from the *academy*. This work is a beginning on that discussion. African-American Muslims scholars are beneficiaries of those interdisciplinary epistemological and axiological world views that emerge from their lived-experiences with academia, professional, and Black-folks *Communiversity* traditions. Our opinions are foundational and essential to an American discourse on Al-Islam and overall Muslim well-being. That conversation regarding the intersection between faith and health, is a necessary and valued one; especially if the view is to supplement the development of effective models of intervention to address challenges that are being faced by the American Muslim community.

In anchoring this work from the vantage point of the Third-wave Humanistic Existential Psychological worldview, as entering a discourse with the Islamic tradition, what is instructive about the text is that it seeks to ground the subject matter both from an epistemological and axiological view regarding the use of terminology. That emphasis on seeking to position or offer utilization of an axiological discourse seems to invite value positions regarding the employ of terminologies *pastoral care* and *compassionate care* considerations; as both science and art. In doing so, what is instructive is that the author lays claim to an embrace of this *compassionate care* model by the referencing to the Quranic verse of *Al-Maun* (The Small Kindnesses). That foundational position then lays claim to the robust discussion that then follows throughout the remainder of this important text. Also, what this claim does is to then cross the threshold into some essential issues that are of relevance in contemporary pubic space conversations.

That attribution is centered on issues of the non-monolithic nature of Muslim ethnic relationships in the United States, the essential places of *Khidmah* (*small kindnesses*- services with a comprehensive flavor), which constitute key components of prayers (the contemplations, the act and the concerns for mindfulness of others) that paves the way for compassionate considerations, safety, human welfare, and eventual justice. According to the scholars of Exegesis (*Tafsir*) in the Islamic tradition, this khidmah opens the doors of bounteous grace and mercy in any society. Hence to be unmindful, neglectful, repulsive, indifferent, and discouraging of people with challenges, the poor, and indigent does invite peril to that society.

Further, the book is a guide text that is to be used in the clinical settings of the mental health profession, to address spiritual care needs, spiritual assessment, family relationships, dietary considerations, and ritual issues that are an integral component of daily faith acts like prayers. This text also invites crucial considerations to what is not approached or adequately referenced in working with Muslim families in these wellness spaces. That point of reference is related to the lived-experiences and embodied-spiritual legacy of what constitute the *Sunna* (verified acts and legacies of how the prophet Muhammad interacted with others). This referencing by the author to this verse of the Qur'an to *small kindnesses* arguably invites those examples for the mental professional to utilize as resources in essentially deciding whether they are in fact treating the corpus of the person with whom you are interacting. Or are they interacting with a spiritual being who is having experiences of consciousness, cognition and affective earthly human wonderings?

Another key essential contribution of this text is the attribution to what is viewed as the *shadow self* in referencing the work of Jung (1933). That association with Jung is valuable due to the fact that it raises critical issues that have been debated in the field of psychology, regarding the advent of humanity. And, it is also concerned with the evolution of the human being. That connection comes at a time in the field when research in anthropology, history, archeology, linguistics, and Human Genome studies now support the view that the human family, Homo Sapiens-Sapiens, did evolve from one human African template; and that the fields do not support notions of speciation. Moreover, as the United States tends to be a micro-reflection of the ethnic composition of the *Global Village culture,* this text can offer some key vignettes that can be useful in a clinical rapprochement with Muslims in this public square discussion.

Additionally, such an association, especially in the field of mental health invites what the noted psychologist Dr. Edwin J. Nichols, sees as the role that the axiological lenses plays in those clinical relationships. That position also sees the lack of a culturally effective professional relationship as being influenced by these axiological lenses in those said interactions. In general, this text can play a role in the faith and intersection discourses that are emerging in the public square. That sense of utility in the mental health field could add value in curriculum development to train and educated emerging mental health professionals, educators, clergy, Rabbis, Imams, healthcare administrators, medical professionals, and the law enforcement sectors.

Overall this text sounds a call for the Indigenous African-American Muslim multi-ethnic people's formations, to become *Deeply Rooted,* as per the position of the Black Muslim Psychology Conference & Muslim Wellness Foundation (2016). The call will then contribute to *Maafa to a Sankofa,* Ani (1997). Dr. Hatim's book is also a necessary value-based, and culturally appropriate activity in the faith and cultural practices traditions of Islam, especially in what is now dubbed by the United Nations' as the *International Decade for the People of African Descent* (2015-2024). Congratulations on bringing forth this important textual resource as contributing to this discussion in the construction of meaning in the American Public Square.

Muhammad A. Al-Rahman, PsyD
Licensed Marriage & Family Therapist, (NY);
National Clinical Fellow (AAMFT);
Certified Master Chaplain (ABCHS),
Board Certified Professional Counselor (BCPC);

Mid-Hudson Valley, NY
September 1, 2016

ACKNOWLEDGEMENTS

I recognize the many people who have contributed to the development of this book. I thank them all. I especially appreciate the encouragement of the late Shaykh Dr. Abdullah Latif Ali and his wife Umm Nur Ali; Shaykh Dr. Ibrahim Abdul-Malik, nonagenarian, colleague, and long-time friend, for his inspiration and editing skills; and the Reverend Dr. Willard Ashely, sounding board and friend for his critical thinking and encouragement. Dr. John Morgan consistently challenged me to write on African American Muslim and pastoral care issues. Dr. Margaret Kornfeld challenged me with her conversations, perspective and approach to pastoral care. Dr. Francine Hernandez and Reverend Carlos Alejandro, CPE Supervisors, helped me to *get out of my own way*. Denise White, Rodney Herring, Charles Ingleton, and Khalilah Aminah Siddiq, substance use disorder/mental health colleagues, provided me feedback and actively listened to my musings and challenges. Imam Abdus-Salaam Musa provided wise counsel and brotherhood throughout my journey. And, I thank Bruce Austin for his emotional support, feedback, and patience. There are many others not herein mentioned who will always have my love and appreciation.

PREFACE

Praise is for Allah. Therefore, I glorify Him and seek His help and forgiveness. And, I seek refuge from my evil inclinations. Whomsoever Allah guides, none mislead; and whomsoever He misleads, none can guide. I bear witness that there is none worthy of worship except Allah, and that Muhammad ibn Abdullah is His servant and Apostle. (Thanawi, n.d, p.25)

Why Write This Book?

The main purpose of this book is to offer suggestions for *Islamic compassionate care* to individual healthcare workers and administrators in related institutions. These professionals may include clinical chaplains, medical personal, counselors, social workers and others. The information may be useful for discussions and in developing training modules in the area of *cultural competency*. Teaching hospitals, schools of social sciences, and clinical pastoral educators are primary targets of this work. Nevertheless, caregiving information herein may be universally useful.

I use the term *pastoral care* in this general discussion. It is a *term of art* used primarily by non-Muslim religious caregivers, specifically Christian chaplains and clergy. Imams and Muslim caregivers find the term *Islamic companionate care* more meaningful. Ordinarily, we do not object to the term pastoral care. The differences between pastoral care and Islamic compassionate care are at the very least epistemological. I address this topic later in the book.

Clinical pastoral care is a particular method of inquiry and exploration used by some caregivers. The objective of the process is to assist a patient or client in arriving at higher and more meaningful levels of well-being. For many Muslims, the sources of inspiration for wellbeing are the religion of Al-Islam, Al-Qur'an, and the recorded traditions (ahadith) of the Prophet Muhammad (pbuh). If non-Muslim caregivers are to be effective and have an authentic relationship with Muslim patients and clients, it is incumbent upon them to be as informed about Al-Islam and Muslims as possible. It is then up to each professional to decide how to incorporate this information into his/her professional understanding, training, and skill base.

Each profession has its own vocabulary for describing the recipient of its services. Hospitals may use the term *patient*. Counselors may use the word *client*. Other professions may use different terms (ASAM, 2013, p.15). For clarity, I chose to limit my description of the recipient of caregiving services to either patient or client, depending on the context of the discussion

Many of my colleagues encouraged me publish. Several of them are professors at leading teaching hospitals, universities, and seminaries. I received encouragement from members of several interfaith organizations. Additionally, a number of forward-thinking Imams and Muslim leaders within the New York City Metropolitan Area, as well as nationally, encouraged this work. I thank all of them for their inspiration and motivation. Any benefit that you receive from this work is the result of Allah's (swt) Mercy. Any mistake that you uncover is mine alone.

Presidential Campaign of 2016 and American Muslims

The country is reeling from the very divisive 2016 Presidential election. During the election, President Donald J. Trump proposed controversial policies concerning Muslim immigration to the US. He suggested the need for increased government surveillance of Muslim individuals and communities. He made references to a possible national registration of Muslims. These proposed policies have the potential to negatively affect the wellness of American Muslim communities. The African American Muslims, American citizens who are the descendants of formerly enslaved forced immigrants, as well as law abiding recent immigrants, now face an unsure and problematic future. The uncertainty of the strategies for implementing such policies can lead to psycho-social-spiritual challenges for Muslims and non-Muslims alike. As clinicians and caregivers, we may be especially impacted in our work in the near future.

The Presidential election campaign of 2016 underscored the

notion of a *national identity*. The election and its associated rhetoric raised several questions: What does it mean to be an American? Is there a test? If so, who should be tested? And, who is really represented in the *American representative democracy*?

Among the voters were some who had a concept of an America that is motivated by an openness and inclusion philosophy (ostensibly the Democrats). There were some other voters who questioned and/or promoted an entitlement to preserving long-held White class privileges and race traditions deeply embedded in the psyche of America (many Republicans). Dr. Nancy Isenberg in her book *White Trash. The 400-year Untold History of Class in America*, to some extent, addressed the entitlement/privilege issue and some of the Republican *deplorables* (referred to by candidate Hillary Clinton in a speech): *Their history starts in the 1500's not the 1900's. It derives from British colonial policies dedicated to resettling the poor, decisions that conditioned American notions of class and left a permanent imprint.* (Isenberg, 2016, p. xiv). The results of the electoral college vote suggested that at least a part of the White community in America felt under sieged by growing numbers of non-White (aka minorities) Americans citizens and immigrants.

By contrast, the notion of an open and inviting America was challenged by Dr. Yusef Kly in his book *The Anti-Social Contract*. In it, he suggested that the Constitution was a *social contract* exclusively for land-owning English men (not women, or others) who established a *settler nation*. Dr. Kly suggested that in fact there exist an *anti-social contract* that covers the remaining inhabitants. He implied that the remaining inhabitants had limited legal standing because they were not a party to the social contract/document:

> …apart from the written portion of the social contract (the U.S. Constitution), there is an unwritten portion, which for lack of a better word we may call the anti-social contract, which determines the significant political relations between the white American majority ethny and the minority ethnies or nations that it governs…. by not having the Africans and Native

Americans represented in the formulation of the Constitution, by not mentioning in the document the slavery of Africans was not acceptable, by speaking as if all Americans were equal and free as they were when obviously some were in chains, and thus leaving open the possibility for an unwritten agreement which accepted the popular notion of the time that Africans and other non-Europeans were not completely human, did not deserve the same rights, were too ignorant or non-Christian to have civilized rights, etc… (Kly, 1989, p.2) [note: Dr. Kly made a distinction between the nation-state and tribal/people nations- see chapter on the Muslim Family]

My political science comments on the 2016 Presidential campaign merely set the tone for addressing the care needed, in light of these events, for the Muslim Community. Additionally, I address psycho-social-spiritual challenges related to America's political and social *shadow self* later in the book. Suffice it to say that the controversy concerning possible forced registration of all Muslims in the United States, uncertainty about the status of undocumented and legal immigrants, election *trash talk,* and other events that might incite violence against Muslims are a concern for professional caregivers to Muslims. This book is a resource for those and others.

My theological thoughts on the 2016 campaign inform me that everything is still in Divine Order. *Allah (swt) is the Best of Planners* (Al-Anfal, 8:30*). And we know that all things work together for good to them that love G-d, to them who are the called according to his purpose (*Romans 8:28).

What Have I Observed?

I offer the comments herein as part of my continuous observation over more than 40 years in ministry and caregiving. It is not my intent to demonize the short-comings of any of particular person, ideology, or organization. Nevertheless, I feel compelled to express the facts as I understand them.

Also, I applaud and encourage the few efforts underway to meet the Muslim Community's spiritual, emotional, and physical needs. My prayer is that more non-Muslim organizations and individuals will begin, with Allah's (swt) guidance, to address the unmet psycho-social-spiritual needs of our community. My comments pertain primarily to the Muslim Communities and clinicians within the New York City Metropolitan Area. Nevertheless, the comments may have universal appeal and application.

Until my recent retirement, for almost 20 years I was active as an Imam with the Admiral Family Circle Islamic Community (Admiral Family). During that time, I studied under the tutelage of the late Shaykh Dr. Abdullah Latif Ali. Shaykh Ali will be remembered (inshallah-if it pleases Allah) as a pioneer in the African American Muslim Community. For many years, he was the General Secretary of the Majlis Ashura (Islamic Leadership Council) of Metropolitan New York. This work developed out of my activities with the Admiral Family. Admiral Family was a Sunni Muslim African American Community. It was founded by Shaykh Ali, and his wife Umm Nur Ali in 1982. It ceased operations in 2013. Admiral Family's activities included offering Friday prayers (Jummah), religious instruction, pre-marriage counselling, and various community services. However, the social forces related to living in a multi-cultural and politically active city such as New York, encouraged the Admiral Family to expand its activities.

In additional to performing his duties as the General Secretary of the Majlis Ashura for over 10 years, Shaykh Ali co-founded the Imam's Council of New York City, as well as The Partnership of Faith in New York City, and the Malik Shabazz (Malcolm X) Human Rights Institute. He and his wife, Umm Nur Ali, spent much of their adult lives in personal development as well as tireless efforts in the establishment and promotion of institutions for the professional development of Imams and Muslim caregivers. My chief roles with the Admiral Family were the director of its Justice Ministry (prisons, jails, and courts); co-founder of our Malik Shabazz Human Rights Institute; Admiral Family's NGO representative to the United Nation Economic and Security Council (ECOSOC); co-director of our Summer Internship Program at the UN Sub-Commission on Human Rights in Geneva, Switzerland; and representative to various interfaith organizations.

During the tragic events of the World Trade Center in 2001, Shaykh Dr. Ali, Umm Nur Ali, Dr. Ibrahim Abdul-Malik and I functioned as Red Cross chaplains. We ministered to Muslims and non-Muslims alike at the Red Cross respite center at the destruction site. Later we gave comfort at Red Cross family assistant centers. The sum total of our experiences, as well as the World Trade Center aftermath and challenges to both the Muslim and non-Muslim Communities of New York City underscored the need for addressing the unmet socio-psycho-spiritual needs in our Muslim Communities.

Furthermore, I write this book to bring to light some of the concerns I have heard and felt from fellow Imams and other Muslims concerning their experiences with Clinical Pastoral Education (CPE) as presently constituted. Most of the comments center upon a certain level of arrogance they stated they have experienced either from CPE supervisors, peer group members, or CPE certifying components. Other comments focused on the stated ignorance of many religious collogues in CPE of basic Islamic principles. Various shades of ignorance often accompanied subtle, and not so subtle acts of hostility. And in conversational subtexts, hardly any of us escaped the *collective guilt* heaped upon us for the misdeeds of some misguided Muslims labeled *terrorists*, or *Islamic fundamentalists*. It appears to many of us that any attempts by Muslims to critically analyze or critically discuss particular religious or political situations related to training seemed to jeopardize further training, evaluations, or Board certification.

There is a paucity of professional educational or general training opportunities offered by Muslim institutions. Indeed, other than masjids, there are very few Muslim institutions in America. We therefore availed ourselves to training offered by Christian and Jewish religious institutions such as hospital chaplaincy programs, or secular public and non-profit organizations. Presently, to my knowledge, there are no Muslim facilities specifically dedicated to clinical training in pastoral care. Similarly, and sadly, to my knowledge, there are no Muslim owned or operated hospital in the United States. Ironically, this is true even though there are any number of celebrated Muslim physicians, surgeons, and administrators in major facilities nationwide.

There are however, several non-profit organizations dedicated to promoting advocacy, and limited professional training. Examples include the American Islamic Indigenous Clinical Pastoral Training (AIICEP) formerly at St. John's Hospital in Queens, NY; Islamic Society of North America (ISNA); Muslim Wellness Foundation (MWF), and Association of Muslim Chaplains (AMC) to name a few.

Chapter Roadmap

The layout and development of the chapters provides the reader with a roadmap to caregiving services for Muslims. *Chapter 1: Fundamentals of Al-Islam* provides a synopsis and brief definition of basic principles of Al-Islam. It discusses faith, belief, and the pillars that support religious praxis. *Chapter 2: Basis of Holistic Pastoral Care for Muslims* explores the philosophical and social challenges that Muslims face in their quest for spiritual wellness. *Chapter 3: Al-Islam. Muslims, and the American Health Care Professionals* addresses specific challenges to the diverse ethnic populations that comprise the Muslim community in America. It explores internal conflicts among various groups. It underscores certain attitudes about the meaning of assimilation. *Chapter 4: Culture/Tradition of the Muslim Family* facilitates an in-depth analysis of discussion on various traditional family values as well as the nature and objective the Muslim society. It addresses issues related to the Muslim GLBTQ individuals. *Chapter 5: Identifying the Spiritual Roots of Terrorism* address psycho-social-spiritual phenomena that contribute to fear, political mischief, the need to belong, and issues of fairness and justice. *Chapter 6: Al-Islam and Clinical Analysis* focuses on the fundamentals of spiritual care, relevant selected psychological and counseling theories, and possible challenges to delivery of care/services. *Chapter 7: The Caregiver and Muslim Spiritual Assessment*, offers a suggestion for spiritual assessment applicable to Muslims as well as 5 summarized brief case studies.

INTRODUCTION

Seest thou one who denies the Judgment (to come)? Then such is the one who repulses the orphan, and encourage not the feeding of the indigent. So woe to the worshipers who are neglectful of their prayers; those who want but to be seen, but refuse (to supply) (even) neighborly needs. (Al-Ma'un, 107, MHE)

The preceding verses from Surah Al-Ma'un discuss the Muslim's responsibility to address basic human needs. The command is not just to meet the needs of Muslims. It speaks about anyone who is our neighbor. This command from Allah (swt) as revealed to the heart of the Prophet Muhammad (pbuh), and codified in Al-Qur'an is also the basis for Islamic Compassionate Care, more commonly referred to as pastoral care.

The purpose of this guide is to provide professionals in the area of caregiving services with information and tools for addressing the well-being and spiritual needs of their Muslim clients. There are already a number of books and documents in the literature that attempt to address some of these needs. Some of these discuss the basic pillars of Al-Islam. Others offer various considerations and approaches to counseling Muslims. My approach to pastoral care and its relationship to Muslims is rooted in the teachings of Al-Islam; i.e. the Al-Qur'an and the ahadith (recorded traditions of the Prophet Muhammad [pbuh]). The end product is a reference that can be used to explore spiritual resources, interventions, outcomes, and measurements for addressing Muslim psycho-social-spiritual needs.

The Muslim Community in the United States is not monolithic. Therefore, realistically, there can be no one-stop-shopping for strategies. One can find Muslims from every part of the world here in the US. Therefore, it is incumbent on each practitioner to do his/her homework on the ethnicity and cultural traditions of his/her charges. The effectiveness of this reference book only can be limited by the knowledge and skills of the one using it. I therefore encourage the user to be open-minded, and willing to see the world, for the moment, through the lens of the Muslims in need of care. I encourage the user to be as competent in his/her discipline as possible; and, rely upon his/her best professional instincts and training.

The clinical suggestions and techniques I offer for achieving the goals of this book are based upon exploration of the *living human document* (Boisen, 1936, p.22) of each Muslim. These techniques will allow the professional (inshallah) to assess the spiritual well-being of the Muslim. They will permit the clinician to journey with him/her as a witness (as-shahid) to improved spiritual health. The clinical assessment criteria in this handbook are founded primarily upon the ideas and strategies of Paul Pruyser (1976).

Which skills are most useful when dealing with Muslim patients? My response is that any and all of them are useful. Skills are only as effective as the practitioner who applies them. The issue at hand is not who applies the skills, but how they are applied and the knowledge-base of the practitioner. It is not enough to say that the person should be culturally competent. That is a basic requirement. The person dealing with Muslim patients also has to be politically astute.

Yes, it is true that a sincerely righteous person full of empathy and professional/cultural competence may possibly be able to minister to anyone including Muslims. Nevertheless, there may be issues of transference and countertransference (appropriate or inappropriate) that should be considered. In light of the events of September 11, 2001, wars with Iraq, present war in Afghanistan, proxy war in Syria, conflict between Israel and Palestine, the uncertainty of a nuclear Iran, and the recent Presidential election, there are possible spiritual issues that can affect the caregiver as well as the client. America has a *shadow self* (Jung, 1933, pg.35) that informs its relationship with Muslims around the world. This shadow may fall as well on caregivers here in the US. It may influence the individual encounter in subtle ways.

While most Muslim patients may be generally receptive to care, please be aware that when you explore feelings, grief, anxiety, or personal issues, you may observe some of the follow concerns:

- *Trust Issues*: thinking or believing that you consider the person a terrorist, knowing a terrorist, or related to one (Islamophobia)
- *Foreign-born Muslims*: a) grief over the loss of friends or relatives to US supported drone bombings in their country of birth; and b) knowing someone detained (sometime questionably) by the US; and questions on US foreign policy
- *African American Muslims*: a) thinking or believing that the caregiver does not consider them *real Muslims*; b) medical malpractice (historic issues of misuse in experiments)
- *Domestic Issues*: a) general family confidentiality; b) male hierarchy as spokesperson(s); and c) western attitudes concerning the role of women
- *Understanding and responding to the cultural difference among Muslim groups*: a) reluctance to shake hands or touch persons of the opposite gender, b) avoiding looking directly into someone's eyes when talking, c) women being alone male medical or housekeeping staff (leave door ajar or open)
- *Issues of ritual purity (Zeno, 1996)*: Salaat (Muslim prayer) is required at least five times a day. Cleanliness is an important component of this process. There is a ritual for washing specific of parts of the body (hands, feet, etc.). There are circumstances under which the ritual may be altered. However, hospitals and the patient's physical condition may present a formidable challenge to an observant Muslims: a) incontinence pads, b) catheter and drainage bags maintenance c) inability to shower following doctor's instruction, and d) blood from IV's, or tubing
- *Gender issues in treatment*: a) preference for same gender medical staff; b) especially, for personal hygiene bathing, catheter insertion, and c) pre-op procedures such as shaving
- *Prayer space*: a) use of the chapel for salaat (prayer) while the room may have uncovered statues and religious images

- *Need for modesty in dress such as*: a) patient gown covering the female body from the neck down with long sleeves that reach the wrists, ankle length, covers back, b) desire to wear hijab (head covering) at all times c) trousers for men (at least covered from the navel to the knees)
- *Dietary issues*: a) request for halaal food (ritualistically slaughtered), b) avoidance of porcine (pork-based) products (including medications)
- *Loss of control personal control*: art of balancing medications for pain or anxiety/depressions and the patient's ability to maintain a clear mind for meeting prayer obligations during salaat (prayer)
- *Medical Ethics*: a) prolonging life artificially, b) pain management, c) abortion issues to save a life, d) organ donors
- *End of life issues*: a) desire for the reading of Surah Ya Sin (Chapter 36) when dying; and b) ritualistic washing of body upon death, c) Janaaza (funeral) prayer and immediate burial.

I have mentioned only a few concerns that Muslims may present in a clinical encounter. Caregiving is an *art* that allows the patient to paint on his/her human cavass with the vibrant colors of wellness. Clinicians are the compassionate witnesses who encourage these masterpieces. May this guide help both the clinician and the client to achieve the wellness of self-actualization.

Chapter 1: Fundamentals of Al-Islam

In the name of Allah, Most Gracious, Most Merciful, praise be to Allah, The Cherisher and Sustainer of the Worlds, Most, Gracious, Most Merciful, Master of the Day of Judgment. Thee do we worship and Thine aid we seek. Show us the straight way, the way of those on whom Thou hast bestowed Thy Grace, those whose portion is not wrath, and who go not astray.

-Al-Fatiha, 1:1-7

There is, however, a strong empirical reason why we should cultivate thoughts that can never be proved. It is that they are known to be useful. Man positively needs general ideas and convictions that will give a meaning to his life and enable him to find a place for himself in the universe ...He can stand the most incredible hardships when he is convinced that they make sense; he is crushed when on top of all his misfortunes, he has to admit that he is taking part in a "tale told by an idiot" ...It is the role of religious symbols to give meaning to the life of man.

-Jung, Man and His Symbols, 1968, p. 76

What is Al-Islam?

In the Arabic language, the word *Islam* has the equivalent meaning to the English concept of submission. The religion is referred to as *Al-Islam*, the submission to the will of Allah (swt). The meaning also implies a sense of surrender, and obedience. One who freely submits his/her will to Allah is referred to as a Muslim. In other words, a Muslim is one who gives himself/herself over to Divine commandments. And again, Al-Islam is the religion.

Who are the Muslims?

The information contained herein is not meant to be exhaustive. It simply is a starting place for those who desire to begin to understand the religion of Al-Islam and American Muslims. Islam is the second largest religion in the world. Statistical information on the number of Muslims world-wide and in the US greatly vary. In 1992, the American Muslim Council (AMC) suggested that there were some 1.3 billion Muslims world-wide; an estimated 5 million in the USA. AMC suggested that the Muslim Community in the United States consisted of the Indigenous African American Muslims (descendants of formerly enslaved Africans forced to immigrate to the US), and Immigrant Muslim Communities (individuals who volunteered to come to the US for social, economic or political reasons). Although estimates vary, the AMC suggested that in the United States the African American Muslims were the largest population at 42%, followed by South Asians 24%, Arabs 12.4%, Africans 5.2%, and others 16.4%. (Nu'man, 1992, p.13). There are an estimated 1,209 masjids in the US (Bagby, 2001), and about 70 masjids in NYC (NYT, 1993).

Muslims are scattered world-wide. Most of the Muslims in the world are Sunni. Sunnis follow closely the principles and practices (sunnah) of the Prophet Muhammad (pbuh) as collected and recorded in the authentic ahadith. Shiites are the second largest Muslim population. For the most part, they have the same theology as Sunnis (belief in One God, prayer, fasting, etc.) but differ in some cultural practices. Shiites are approximately 10-15% of the world-wide Muslim Community.

Islamic Faith and Worship

La illaha illallah, there is no deity/god except Allah. This statement is an expression of the Oneness of Allah (*tawhid*). Allah has no partners or helpers. He is not in need of anything. He alone is worthy of worship. Additionally, it is the duty of every Muslim to accept this principle. Indeed, this point-of-faith is what distinguishes Al-Islam (the religion) and Muslims (the practitioners) from other religions and their adherents. The concept of faith is based upon the revelations of the Holy Qur'an as follows:

> Say, He is Allah, the One, Allah the Eternal, Absolute. He begetteth not, nor is He begotten, And there is none like unto Him. (Al-Iklas, 112)

Allah (swt) is The Unseen, Unprovable, and Supernatural. He is the Most High (*A'la*), the Creator (*Al-Khaliq*) and Sustainer (*Ar-Rahim*) of the heavens and earth. Allah (swt) is far beyond human comprehension, beyond even the furthest reaches of human imagination. He is beyond space and time. Therefore, our relationship to Him is one of unconditional confidence and trust, beyond human reason. This faith is expressed in surah Al-Baqarah as follows:

> Allah! There is no god but He, the Living, the Self-subsisting, Supporter of all. No slumber can seize Him nor sleep. His are all things in the heavens and on earth. Who is there can intercede in His presence, except as He permitteth? He knoweth what (appeareth to His creatures as) before, or after, or behind him. Nor shall they compass aught of His knowledge except as He willeth. His throne doth extend over the heavens and the earth, and He feeleth no fatigue in guarding and preserving them, for He is the Most High, the Supreme (in glory). (Al-Baqarah, 2:255)

This one-point-of-faith is not rational. It is supra-rational. It cannot be induced or deduced. It is not based on a theorem, hypothesis, speculation or logic. Faith concerns itself with unconditional love, trust and confidence in Allah (swt), and for some, fear. Faith is a gift from Allah (swt), one to be cherished, developed through belief, and, it can be lost through ingratitude. The worship of anything other than Allah(swt) can lead to spiritual distress, grief, and/or forms of punishment. This is expressed in surah Al-Baqarah:

> Yet there are men who take (for worship) others beside Allah, as equal (with Allah). For they love them as they should love Allah. But those of faith are overflowing in their love for Allah. If only the unrighteous could see, behold, they would see the punishment: that to Allah belongs all power, and He will strongly enforce the punishment. (2:165)

Faith can be increased or decreased, but only as Allah (swt) wills. It is by His mercy (rahman) that we benefit from faith. He pours it into us as into a glass or a bowl. He removes it from us when the vessel, our being rejects faith. And if we go astray, Allah (swt) may remove himself and His gift from us.

> Those who believe, and then reject faith, then believe (again), and (again) reject faith, and go on increasing in un-belief, Allah will not forgive them, nor guide them on the way. (An-Nisaa, 4:137)

This verse (ayah) reminds us that rejection of faith is a rejection of a gift from Allah (swt). Rejection of faith will increase un-belief. Al-Qur'an assures us that Allah (swt) will not forgive the rejection of faith, an action that further leads to the increase in un-belief. With this unbelief comes the promise of no forgiveness and misguidance. Implied in the ayah is the hope that Allah will be merciful. So, if after the initial rejection of faith, the believer repents and experiences an increase in belief, and does not again reject, he/she will be rewarded with blessings and grace from Allah (swt) who is the source of all faith.

Islamic Points of Belief

Belief in Al-slam is experiential. In general, we believe in part because we accept and internalize something we experienced. This can be a thing we heard, saw, read, or thought. This becomes the evidence that we accept as reality. Belief can be a result of rational or irrational thinking which we accept as truth. Basic Islamic points of belief are traditionally listed are as follows:

- *Belief in Allah The Supreme, The Merciful, Compassionate*: Allah is the only deity, and alone is worthy of praise. His mercy and bounties are endless. He is without partners, and nothing is done without His permission.

- *Belief in all the Prophets and Messengers of Allah (swt)*: Prophets are human beings chosen by Allah (swt) as vehicles through whom Holy Scriptures descend. The first revelation came through Prophet Adam (as) the ancestor all human beings. The last revelation came through Prophet Muhammad (pbuh). Al-Qur'an also mentions that Allah (swt) sent revelations through other prophets, *e.g.* Ibrahim (Abraham), Dawud (David), Musa (Moses). Isa (Jesus), and others not mentioned by name (peace be upon them all).

As Muslims, we make no distinction among any of Allah's (swt) prophets. They were men and women, selected and prepared for this position. They were Allah's (swt) filters through whom His message could be cleanly transmitted:

> For We assuredly sent amongst every peoples a messenger (with the command), "Serve Allah and eschew evil." Of the people were some whom Allah guided, and some on whom error became inevitably (established). So travel through the earth, and see what was the end of those who denied (the Truth). (An-Nahl, 16:36)

The Qur'an makes a distinction between the role of prophets and messengers. Some individuals were both. Examples of prophets include: Prophet Muhammad (pbuh) (Al-Ahzab, 33:40); Prophet Isa (Jesus) [as] (Maryam, 19:30); and Prophet Ibrahim (Abraham) [as] (Maryam, 19:41). Examples of those who were messengers include: Rasul Elias (Elijah) [as] (As-Saffat, 37:123); and Rasul Yunus (Jonah) [as] (As-Saffat, 37:139). Prophets delivered their messages in the language of their people, so that they would be clearly understood. The message from Allah (swt) to the Arabs was impressed upon the heart of Prophet Muhammad (Ash-Shu'araa, 192-195), and spoken in the language of his people. His coming was foretold in the Hebrew Scriptures in the book of Deuteronomy (Chapter 18:14-20, Baker).

- *Belief in Angel Beings*: Angels are beings created from light. They have no free-will. They only perform duties as commanded by Allah (swt). Angels do however have the ability to reason. This means that they rationalize, and weigh information given to them. There are no fallen angels in Islamic theology. In certain respects, humans have an advantage over angels. Allah (swt) ordered them to bow down to Prophet Adam [as] (Al-Baqarah, 2:34). Angels have been used to communicate divine revelations to humankind. For example, Angel Gabriel (as) brought the news of Isa's (as) impending birth to Maryam [as] (Mary). Al-Qur'an informs us that some angels have responsibilities such as guardians to paradise and the hellfire. An example of the angels' ability to rationalize and question follows:

    Behold, thy Lord said to the angels, "I will create a vicegerent on earth." They said, "Wilt Thou place therein one who makes mischief and shed blood, whilst we do celebrate Thy praises and glorify Thy holy (name)?" He said: "I know what you know not." (Al-Baqarah, 2:30)

The angels entered into a dialogue with Allah (swt) over the nature of human beings. They questioned as to why a creature that sheds blood, and creates mischief should exist. Allah (swt) responded by suggesting that there is some knowledge that is beyond the wisdom of angels. This concept of not being able to understand Allah's (swt) plan for human beings is fundamental to the religion of Islam. Allah (swt) is the Best Planner, The Best Knower. By Allah's (swt) command, angels give inspiration to human beings. Al-Qur'an confirms this as follows:

> He doth send down His angels with inspiration of His command, to such of His servants as He pleaseth, (saying): "Warn (man) that there is no god but I. So do your duty unto Me. (An-Nahl, 16:2)

> • *Belief in Jinn Beings*: Jinn beings are created from smokeless fire (Al-Hijr, 15:27). In Al-Qur'an, jinn are described as rational beings who can hear, discern, appreciate truth, and can correct sinful behavior (Al-Jinn, 72:2). Among the jinn there are those who submit to the will of Allah (swt), and those who do not. Therefore, jinn will ultimately be held accountable, similar to humans, on The Day of Judgment. Contrary to popular beliefs, not all jinn are inherently devilish or evil.

Jinn also were required to submit to human beings. They all did, except the Devil. He is better known as Iblis, one of the shayateen (devils). The name Iblis implies one who is proud or haughty. The word shaytan is used to refer to someone who rebels against Allah's (swt) commandments. It also connotes the idea of perversity or enmity (Note 52, MHE, p.52). The story is recounted as follows:

> Behold, We said to the angels, "Prostrate to Adam!" They prostrated except Iblis. He was one of the jinn, and he broke the command of his Lord. Will ye then take him and his progeny as protectors rather than Me? And they are enemies to you! Evil would be the exchange for the wrong-doers. (Al-Kuhf, 18:50)

Allah (swt) gives protection and mercy to those who reject the shayateen. There is hell to pay for those who follow them instead of their Lord.

> • *Belief in the Day of Judgment and the Hereafter*: This is the belief that man's life is not without a meaningful end, and that death is certain. One day, life as we understand it will cease to exist. Each person will be held accountable for his/her actions. Allah (swt) will confront everyone with a record of deeds. Then, depending on the balance of evil and good deeds, Allah (swt) will determine whether to grant the person the reward of paradise or the punishment of hell.

When the earth is shaken to her (utmost) convulsion, and the earth throws up her burdens (from within), and man cries (distressed) "What is the matter with her?" On that Day will she declare her tidings. For that thy Lord will have given her inspiration... On that Day will men proceed in groups sorted out, to be shown their deeds that they (had done). Then shall anyone who has done an atom's weight of good, see it! And anyone who has done an atom's weight of evil, shall see it. (Al-Zilzal, 99:1-8)*Belief in Predetermination*: Not only is death certain, but, like birth, it is predestined to occur at a specific point or time. This date cannot be changed, and is known only to Allah (swt). Predestination means that everything that does or could occur throughout time is known to Allah (swt). Accordingly, this implies that creatures have predisposed natures. This fact can be a little troubling and a great mystery. It can challenge the concept of freewill. Nevertheless, there are some people as well as jinn who are destined for Hell. However, Allah (swt) is the Best Knower about such things.

Evil as the example are people who reject Our signs, and wrong their own souls. Whom Allah guides, he is on the right path. Whom He rejects from His guidance, such are the persons who lose! Many are the jinns and men We have made for hell. They have hearts wherewith they understand not, eyes wherewith they see not, and ears wherewith they hear not. They are like cattle. – nay more misguided, for they are heedless (of warning). (Al-A'raf, 7:179)

Islamic Worship (Ibadah) System

Beliefs are expressed as a part of the Islamic worship system (praxis). The religion of Al-Islam consists of a unique set of religious acts. They include but are not limited to the following:

> • *Bearing witness to the Oneness of Allah (swt), and to the Messengership of Muhammad (pbuh)*: This profession is usually made in the form *la illaha ilallah, Muhammadan rasulu Allah*, (There is no god but Allah, Muhammad is a messenger of Allah). The Qur'an mentions this point as follows:

> And they have been commanded no more than this: to worship Allah, offering Him sincere devotion, being true (in faith), to establish prayer, and to give zakat; and that is the religion right and straight. (Al-Baiyina, 98:5), and

> Muhammad is not the father of any of your men, but (he is) The Messenger of Allah and the Seal of the Prophets; and Allah is full of knowledge of all things. (Al-Ahzab, 33:40)

> • Performing the five daily prayers: Morning (*Fajr*); Noon (*Dhuhr*); Afternoon (*Asr*); Evening (*Maghrib*); Night (*Isha*): Allah (swt) created all living things for the purpose of serving Him. Prayer keeps man focused on Allah (swt). It prevents him from worshiping everything else (*e.g.* himself, money, sex) by establishing regular religious acts. Through these means, humans keep themselves in tune with the universal theme of creation.

Muslims are required to perform formal prayers (*salaat*) five times daily, facing towards the Ka'ba in Mecca. The Ka'ba is the traditional temple build by Prophet Ibrahim (as) and his son Ismael (as). Muslims are also required to attend the Friday congregational prayers (*salaat-ul-jumah*). Salaat is a ritual, performed according to a prescribed sequence of physical movements and intensions.

Before a believer approaches salaat, he/she must achieve a state of ritualistic purity. This is accomplished by performing an act of ablution called *wudu*. For the believer, wudu is more than mere washing of the appropriate body parts. It is performed with a prayerful intention and attitude in preparation for the impending communication with the Almighty.

- *Paying the religious tax (zakat)*: Zakat is often mistakenly translated as charity. Its root word has the meaning *to purify*. Muslims are required to pay a specified amount of tax to the Islamic community or state in which he or she is a member. This exemplifies the fact that a Muslim must be a *formal member* of a Muslim collective in order to meet his/her religious obligation. As stated, the payment of zakat not only economically supports the community, but acts to purify the soul of the payer.

- *Keeping the fast of the Holy Month of Ramadan*: Muslims are required to fast each day during the month of Ramadan, from dawn to dusk. The fast requires that the person refrain from all food and drink (including water), and from all sexual activity during the daylight hours. The much deeper meaning of the fast is spiritual. It is an opportunity for believers to deepen their spiritual practices, and to emerge from the month-long involvement better equipped to face the challenges of the ensuing year.

- *Making a pilgrimage to the Holy City of Mecca*: During the Hajj season, Muslims are required to perform the pilgrimage to the Holy City of Mecca -- at least once in a lifetime. The pilgrimage is one of the five pillars of Islam. Although the Hajj is obligatory on all Muslims, exemptions are made for those persons who are not physically, mentally, and/or economically equipped to make the journey.

In earlier times, Hajj was a long and often dangerous journey due to the hardships and uncertainties of travel. Today, jumbo jets cover the distance to Mecca in a matter of hours, from any part of the world. They also offer a measure of comfort that was not possible to earlier pilgrims.

Today, upwards of three million people assemble for the pilgrimage to visit the House of Allah. With adequate preparation, however, and the exercise of reasonable caution, it is entirely possible for an individual to negotiate all of the obligatory activities in safety and with proper solemnity. The Qur'an mentions the Hajj in these words:

Say: Allah speaketh the truth. Follow the religion of Ibrahim, the sane in faith. He was not of the pagans. The first House (of worship) appointed for men was that at Bakka (Mecca), full of blessing and of guidance for all the worlds. In it are signs manifest. The station of Ibrahim, whoever enters it attains security. Pilgrimage thereto is a duty men owe to Allah, those who can afford the journey. But, if any deny faith, Allah stands not in need of any of His creatures. (Al-Imran, 3:97-97)

• *Engaging in Jihad (Struggle, Striving, and Fighting)*: Humans worship Allah (swt) in compliance to His will and purpose for creation. That is, to become Allah's (swt) deputy on earth. Man also has to create state (theocratic or democratic) in which Allah's laws are practiced. This struggle may sometimes be physical. At other times, the struggle can be against the self for obedience (jihad-ul-nafs). This is usually considered the greater jihad.

• *Avoiding Certain Actions that are Forbidden by Islam*: Engaging in these forbidden activities is likely to cause religious stress, grief, mental and/or spiritual challenges. Forbidden are:

- *All kinds of intoxicating wines, liquors, and spirits (Al-Baqarah, 2:219)*; the meat and products of swine (pork, bacon, ham, lard); wild animals that use claws or teeth to kill their victims (tigers, wolves, leopards); or birds of prey (hawks, vultures, crows); rodents, reptiles, worms and the like; dead animals and birds that are not slaughtered properly. (Al-Baqarah, 2:173)

- *All forms of gambling and vain sports* (Al-Baqarah, 2:19); all sexual relations out of wedlock (marriage contract), and all manners of talking, walking, looking, and dressing in public that may instigate temptation, arouse desire, stir suspicion, or indicate immodesty and indecency.

The Glorious Qur'an

Muslims believe that Al-Qur'an (The Recitation) is the last sacred book and final revelations from Allah (swt) to mankind. The Qur'an identifies itself by many names. Some of these include: Al-Kitab (The Book), Al-Dhikir (The Reminder), Al-Ruh (The Spirit), Ar-Rahman (The Mercy), and Al-Haqq (The Truth). Al- Qur'an consists of 114 Chapters (Surahs), 30 parts (ajza), and 6247 verses (ayat) (Ali, 1995, i-ii).

The angel Gabril (as) referred to as The Holy/Truthful Spirit, directly transmitted the message into the heart of the Prophet Muhammad. The first revelation occurred during the month of Ramadan on Lait Al-Qadr (The Night of Power).

> Verily this is a revelation from the Lord of the Worlds; with it came down The Truthful Spirit to thy heart that thou mayest admonish in a perspicuous Arabic tongue. Without doubt it is (announced) in the revealed Books of former peoples. (Al-Shu'ara, 26:192-196)

Al-Qur'an summarized guidance for correct belief and practice offered to human beings as follows:

> A.L.M. This is the Book. In it is guidance sure, without doubt, to those who fear Allah, who believe in the Unseen, are steadfast in (establish) Prayer, and spend out of what we have provided for them, and who believe in the Revelation sent to thee, and sent before thy time, and (in their hearts) have assurance of the Hereafter. They are on (true guidance) from their Lord, and it is these who will prosper. (Al-Baqarah, 2:2-5)

Allah (swt) revealed the message of Al-Qur'an over a period of 23 years. Al-Qur'an confirms Allah's (swt) earlier communications through prophets and messengers. The guidance provided suggestions for authentic religious practice, acceptable behavior, and methods for building responsible and accountable communities.

> It is He who sent down to thee (step-by-step) in truth, the Book confirming what went before it. And, He sent down the Torah (of Moses) and the Gospel (of Jesus) before this, as a guide to mankind, and He sent down the Criterion (of judgment between right and wrong). Then those who reject Faith in the Signs of Allah will suffer the severest Chastisement; and Allah is Exalted in Might, Lord of Retribution. (Al-Imran, 3:3-4)

Al-Qur'an's provides spiritual direction. It offers consolation for general sadness, clinical depression, anxiety, and other diseases of the spirit.

> Oh mankind! there hath come to you an admonition from your Lord and a healing for the diseases in your heart; and for those who believe, a Guidance and a Mercy. (Yunus, 10:57)

It provides the path to the light of well-being and spiritual wholeness.

> A.L.R. A Book which We have revealed unto thee, in order that thou mightiest lead mankind out of the depths of darkness into light-by the leave of their Lord- to the Way of (Him) the Exalted in Power, Worthy of all Praise! (Ibrahim, 14:1)

In contemporary terms, the Qur'an can be viewed as an operator's manual for mankind. It shows how to keep the entire mind, body and soul in perfect working order, consistent with Allah's *(swt)* will and His Guidance. It is for those who keep their duty to Allah *(swt)*, believe in the unseen, consistently persevere in prayer, and spend out of their resources according to the dictates of Allah *(swt)*. And, it is for those who believe in this revelation and other divine revelations sent before it, and who are assured of the afterlife.

In effect, the Qur'an can be seen as a structure for a *pyscho-social* and *psycho-spiritual* analysis. The Book is especially useful for those who are seeking spiritual healing and inspiration. It helps them to maintain a balance (mizan), while they are progressing on the path of righteousness, as ordained by Allah. It explains that the prophets Isa (as), (Ibrahim) (as) and others were righteous believers who submitted to the will of the Allah (swt). By definition, one who submits himself/herself to the will to Allah (swt) is a Muslim. Muslims believe that Al-Qur'an contains the final revelations from Allah (swt).

The Importance of Covenants in Al-Islam

Definition of Covenant

According to Webster's Dictionary (1966), the word *covenant* is defined as: *A binding and solemn agreement to do, or keep from doing a specific thing.* In other words, an agreement is something to which you say *yes*; something to which you give your word, pledge, or commitment. A covenant also implies that there is a binding authority to mediate disputes. In the covenant in Al-Islam, Allah (swt) promises that if we are faithful to Him, He will be faithful to us: *Then do ye remember Me, I will remember you. Be grateful to Me, and reject not Faith.* (Al Baqarah, 2:152).

Allah has encouraged the believers to make contracts, a form of a covenant, among themselves:

> O ye who believe! When ye deal with each other, in transaction involving future obligations in a fixed period of time, reduce them to writing. Let a scribe write down faithfully, as between the parties. Let not the scribe refuse to write, as Allah has taught him, and disdain not to reduce to writing (your contract) for a future period, whether it be small of big. It is juster [sic] in the sight of Allah, more suitable as evidence, and more convenient to prevent doubts among yourselves. But if it be a transaction which ye carry out on the spot among yourselves, there is no blame on you if ye reduce it not to writing. (Al-Baqarah, 2:282)

Muslims make a daily covenant with Allah (swt). Muslims follow the guidance and dictates of The Book. In return, Allah (swt) promises success in this life and the next as cited earlier (Al-Baqarah, 2:2-5). When a non-Muslims embraces the religion of Al-Islam, he/she makes a covenant called a *shahad*a. It can be very brief or extensive depending on the desires of a specific community. The shahada should include but is not limited to: *ash-shadu an la ilaha illa-llah* (I bear witness that nothing deserves to be worshipped except Allah) and *ash-shadu anna Muhammadan Rasulu-llah* (I bear witness that Muhammad is the Messenger of Allah). (Zeno, 1996, p.89).

Covenant with Prophet Adam (as)

A covenant was made with Prophet Adam (as) after he and his mate rejected Allah's (swt) guidance. They breached the covenant and fell from a state of Grace (closeness with Allah) by disobeying.

> And, We said: "O Adam! Dwell thou and thy wife in the garden; and eat of the bountiful things therein as (where and when) ye will; but approach not this tree, or ye run into harm and

transgression." Then did Satan make them slip from the (garden) and get them out of a state (of felicity) in which they had been. And we said "Get down, all (ye people) with enmity between yourselves. On earth will be your dwelling place, and your means of livelihood, for a time." (Al-Baqarah, 2:35-36)

After the disobedience, Allah offered a covenant (agreement for obtaining His mercy) as follows:

We said: "Get ye down from here! And if, as is sure, there comes to you guidance from Me, whosoever follows My guidance, on them shall be no fear, nor shall they grieve. but those who reject faith and belie our signs, they shall be companions of the fire; they shall abide therein." (Al-Baqarah, 2:38-39)

Covenant with Prophet Ibrahim (as) and His Descendants

Allah began by establishing Prophet Ibrahim (as) as an *Imam* (leader).

And remember that Abraham was tried by his Lord with certain commandments which he fulfilled. He said: "I will make thee an Imam to the people." He pleaded: "And also (Imams) for my offspring." He answered: "But My promise is not within the reach of evil-doers." (Al-Baqarah, 2:124)

The designation *Imam to the people* raised Prophet Ibrahim and his descendants to the status of leadership for humankind. The Hebrew prophets (leaders) who descended from Prophets Ibrahim (as) and Isaq (as) are recorded in the Torah, a Jewish Holy Book.

Covenant with Prophet Ishmael (as)

The Prophet Ishma'il (as) is mentioned in both the Hebrew Scriptures as well as Al-Qur'an. He was the elder son of Prophet

Ibrahim (as). His mother was Hagar (as), the second wife of Prophet Ibrahim (as) (Beresit, 16:3). One tradition states that she originally was a member of high standing in Pharaoh's court. A misunderstanding ensued between Pharaoh and Prophet Ibrahim (as) over his wife Sa'rai (as) (Beresit,12:18-29). As a part of Pharaoh's apology, Hagar (as) became the equivalent to a lady-in-waiting (handmaiden) to Sa'rai (as) (Beresit, 16:1). Subsequently, for apparent domestic reasons, Hagar (as) and Prophet Isma'il (as) separated from Prophet Ibrahim (as). Prophet Isma'il (as) later became an Imam (leader) of his own people (Beresit, 16:10).

> Also mention in the Book (the story of) Isma'il. He was (strictly) true to what he promised, and he was a messenger (and) a prophet. He used to enjoin on his people prayer and zakat, and he was most acceptable in the sight of his Lord. (Maryam, 19:54)

The covenant also included making provision for the Hajj:

> Remember We made the House a place of assembly for men, and a place of safety. And take ye the station of Abraham as a place of prayer. And We covenanted with Abraham and Isma'il that they should sanctify My house for those who compass it round, or use it as a retreat, or bow, or prostrate themselves (therein in prayer). (Al-Baqarah, 2:125)

Covenant with Prophet Muhammad (pbuh)

Allah (swt) sent the Prophet Muhammad (pbuh) as a mercy to mankind. He was a reformer charged to bring monotheists back to the purity of the worship of the One God. Allah (swt) needed no partners or assistance. His covenant with the Prophet (pbuh) and his community (ummah) suggested that when they follow his commandments, they will be successful as a people and find peace and security:

> Allah has promised, to those among you who believe and work righteous deeds, that He will, of a surety, grant them

> in the land inheritance (of power), as He granted it to those before them; that He will establish in authority their religion -the one which He has chosen for them; and, that He will change their state, after the fear in which they lived, to one of security and peace. They will worship Me (alone) and not associate aught with Me. If any do reject faith after this, they are rebellious and wicked. (An-Nur, surah 24:55)

Prophet Muhammad (pbuh) was sent as a mercy and messenger to all mankind:

> Verily in this (Qur'an) is a message for people who would (truly) worship Allah. We sent thee not, but as a mercy for all creatures. Say: "What has come to me by inspiration is that your God is One God; will ye therefore bow to His will (in Islam)? Surely, Muhammad is a prophet of Allah." (Al-Anbiyaa, 21:106-108)

Responsible Actions Covered by the Divine Covenant

As a part pf the Divine covenant, humans have responsibilities. They include worship and loyalty. Success and prosperity come from fulfilling the covenant:

> Oh ye people! Worship your Guardian Lord Who created you and those who came before you that ye may become righteous. Who has made the earth your couch, and the heavens your canopy; and sent down rain from the heavens; and brought forth therewith fruits for your sustenance; then set not rivals unto Allah when you know (the truth). (Al-Baqarah, 2:21-22)

There are consequences from breaking the covenant:

> Those who break Allah's Covenant after it is ratified and who sunder what Allah has ordered to be joined, and do mischief on earth; these cause loss (only) to themselves. (Al-Baqarah, 2:27)

Success comes with honoring and maintaining the covenant:

> Those who believe (in the Qur'an) and those who follow the Jewish (scriptures), and the Christians, and the Sabeans, who believe in Allah and the Last Day and work righteousness, shall have their reward with their Lord, and on them shall be no fear, nor shall they grieve. (Al-Maida, 5:69)

The covenant is confirmed by the remembrance of Allah (swt):

> Then do remember Me, I will remember you. Be grateful to Me, and reject not faith. Oh ye who believe! Seek help with patient perseverance and pray; for God is with those who patiently persevere. (Al-Baqarah, 2:152-153)

Summary Comments

The purpose of this Chapter is to give the non-Muslim caregiver a basic understanding of fundamentals of Al-Islam. The objective is to supply material that can be used to supplement the clinical and spiritual assessment process, development of treatment plans, and give insight into the mind and soul of the Muslim client/patient. There are fundamental differences among the monotheistic religions, Al-Islam, Judaism, and Christianity. The historic manner in which they have behaved towards one another appears antithetical to their basic principles. Yet, their creeds contain principles of love, charity, kindness, and caring.

Chaplains, CPE educators, pastoral care providers, healthcare workers, social workers, and others have the moral responsibility to rise above parochial differences. Professor Miroslav Volf of Yale University witnessed many years of war and religious conflict in the former Yugoslavia. I agree with his assertions as they apply to caregiving. He aptly described religious challenges he observed. I mention two:

> Christians and Muslims worship one and the same God, the only God. They understand God's character partially differently, but the object of their worship is the same. I reject the idea that Muslims worship a different God than do Jews

and Christians.

He continued:

> What matters is not whether you are Christian or Muslims or anything else; instead, what matters is whether you love God with all your heart...I reject making religious belonging and religious labels more significant than allegiance to the one true God. (Volf, 2011, pp. 14-15)

I have offered a brief description of the fundamental of Al-Islam. The patients will bring their individual understanding and Islamic experience to an encounter. It is my prayer that readers will be able to use some of the material to enhance their clinical skills and cultural competence when addressing Muslims in need of caregiving.

Chapter 2: Basis of Holistic Pastoral Care for Muslims

Actions are but by intentions and every man shall have what he intended. Thus, he whose migration was for Allah and His Messenger, his immigration was for Allah and His Messenger, and he whose migration was to achieve some worldly benefit or to take some woman in marriage, his migration was for that which he migrated.

-Prophet Muhammad, Forty Hadith, No.1

Religion has clearly performed great services for human civilization. It has contributed much towards the taming of the asocial instincts. But not enough. It has ruled human society for many thousands of years and has had time to show what it can achieve. If it had succeeded in making the majority of mankind happy, in comforting them, in reconciling them to life and making them into vehicles of civilization, no one would dream of attempting to alter the existing conditions. But what do we see instead? We see that an appallingly large number of people are dissatisfied with civilization and unhappy in it, and feel it as a yoke which must be shaken off, and that these people either do everything in their power to change that civilization, or else go so far in their hostility to it that they will have nothing to do with civilization or with a restriction of instinct.

-Freud, Sigmund, The Future of an Illusion, 1961, p.47

The Meaning and Purpose of the Human Soul (Nafs)

Allah (swt) created human beings to worship (serve) Him, and Him alone (Az-Zariyat, 51:56). During the creation of Prophet Adam (as) and his mate, Allah (swt) fashioned and filled them with essence from Himself (Al-Hijr, 15:29). In the Al-Qur'an, this essence is referred to as *ruh*. It is most often translated as spirit. Not much is known about the true nature of the ruh. This is confirmed by the Holy Qur'an: *They ask thee concerning the Spirit. Say, The Spirit is of the command of my Lord of knowledge. It is only a little that is communicated to you (Oh men!)* (Bani Isra-il, 17:85).

Next, there is the subject of the *soul* of human beings. The Arabic word *nafs* is most often translated as soul. For the sake of this discussion, the ruh is the essence/breath that comes from Allah (swt). The nafs (soul) is that part of the human that lives, dies, and which must be judged. It is distinct from the ruh (spirit). Al-Qur'an explains this difference as follows: *But He fashioned him in due portion and breathed into him of His Spirit. And He gave you (the facilities of) hearing and sight and understanding; little thanks do ye give*! (As-Sajda, 32:9)

My limited understanding of the relationship is as follows: The human body is the physical vehicle which carries the ruh (essence) and the nafs (soul). And the *mind* is the result of the interaction/realization between the ruh (essence) and the soul (nafs). It manifests as awareness and has *free-will*. The behavior realized and exhibited by this interaction can be observed as *personality*. That is, the quality of character which emerges from choices (free-will) made by the mind. The personality reflects the quality and state of the *heart* of the human being. The resulting behavior can express a righteous *heart at peace with Allah* (Al-Fajr, 89:27). Or, the behavior can reflect a *heart that is diseased* [has a spiritual disorder] (Al-Baqarah 2:10). Humans who reject Allah's (swt) Guidance (Al-Qur'an) are defined as the unbelievers (kafiroon).

A mind (ruh and nafs) at peace is in harmony, and obedience to Allah's (swt) laws and precepts. The mind has the ability to discern truth from falsehood. It knows in its deepest core, that which is right (Al-Anfal, 8:29). Human beings are capable of great acts of goodness, as well as acts of viciousness and deprivation. There are various types of nafs. Al-Qur'an described them as follows:

- Na*fs Al-Ammarah*: The Commanding Soul; those souls inclined towards evil.

Yet I do not absolve myself (of blame). The (human) soul certainly incites evil; unless my Lord do bestow His mercy; but surely my Lord is Ort-Forgiving, Most Merciful. (Yusuf, 12:53)

- *Nafs Al-Lawammah*: The Blaming Soul; those souls possessing moral consciences.

I do swear by the Resurrection Day and I do swear by the self-reproaching soul. Does man think that We cannot assemble his bones? Nay, We are able to put together in perfect order the very tips of his fingers. But man wished to do wrong (even) in the time in front of him. (Al-Qiyamat, 75:2-5)

- *Nafs Al-Mulhamah:* The Inspired Soul; possess self-knowledge and an understanding of what is sin, piety and righteous deeds, makes choices accordingly.

By the Sun and his glorious splendor; by the moon as she follows him, by the day as it shows up (the sun's) glory, by the night as it conceals it, by the firmament and the (wonderful) structure, by the earth and its (wide) expense, by the soul and the proportion and order given to it, and its inspiration as to its wrong and its right, truly he succeeds that purifies it, and he fails that corrupts it. (Ash-Shams, 91:1-10)

- *Nafs Al-Mutma'inna*: The Satisfied/Resolved Soul; those souls inspired by piety to dedication to the Oneness of Allah (*tawhid*).

(To the righteous will be said) "Oh (thou) soul in (complete) rest and satisfaction." (Al-Fajr, 89:27), and

- *Nafs Al-Radiyah*: The Well-Pleased/Adjusted Soul; contend with self; seeing best in everything, and all circumstances.

Come back thou to thy Lord well pleased (thyself) and well-pleasing unto Him. Enter thou then, among mu devotees! Yes, enter thou my heaven. (Al-Fajr, 89:28)

Only Allah (swt) knows fully the reason He created human beings. He knows the purpose for endowing them with free will and rationality. In His Mercy, He gave humans a road map, a guide, a protocol for living the best lives possible. This guide is the Al-Qur'an, and His final messenger is Prophet Muhammad (pbuh). The key to good mental and spiritual health for a Muslim is to follow the guidance, the straight path (*mustalkeem*) described in Al-Qur'an. Life is as test and challenge to the soul. Allah (swt) will be the final judge:

We have indeed created man in the best molds. Then do We abase him (to be) the lowest of the low, except such as believe and do righteous deeds; for they shall have a reward unfailing. What then can after this make you deny the Last Judgment? Is not Allah the Wisest of Judges? (At-Tin, 95:4-8)

Selected Spiritual Challenges within the Muslim Community

Introduction

For certain, there were unmet needs in the Muslim community before the tragic events of September 11, 2001, before the wars with Iraq and Afghanistan, before detainment of Muslims in Guantánamo Bay in Cuba, or before the non-Muslim community backlash. However, these events have heavily underscored and heightened these unmet need.

My own work with the Admiral Family Circle Islamic Community (Admiral Family) included activities to address some of these challenges. For example, we created a *Justice Ministry*. We chose to call our efforts a Justice Ministry instead of a Prison Ministry. The main reason was because we addressed the spiritual needs of more than just the inmates. We ministered to attorneys, court officers, judges, and family members as well. We even held several discussions with New York State court officials on the feasibility/possibility of the State instituting courtroom chaplains. In my opinion and observation, this is an area that is sorely missing caregiving in general. A lack of State or non-profit funding appears to be the major deterrent.

In the year 2000, the United Nations Economic and Social Council (ECOSOC) awarded the Admiral Family *Special* consultative status for its humanitarian work with Muslim and non-Muslim communities. Annually, Admiral Family participated in meetings of the United Nations Sub-Commission on the Promotion and Protection of Human Rights in Geneva, Switzerland. Admiral Family took an active role in meetings at the UN New York headquarters, joining in the UN's efforts to develop an *Internal Convention on the Rights of People with Disabilities*.

After the attack in York City on the World Trade Center, Admiral Family became intensely involved with both Muslims and non-Muslims in response. We coordinated compassionate care activities with Imams at several of the largest Muslim communities; lectured on techniques for responding to *critical incidents*; co-sponsored and participated in the only Muslim Disaster Conference offered in the city; and received training in palliative care (death and dying), critical incident stress management, and in care-for-caregivers. Four of our members became Red Cross chaplains. We worked at the *Respite Centers* ministering to uniformed personnel and other rescue workers. Additionally, we attended to the spiritual needs of families of victims at the *Family Assistance Center*.

Selected Roles of the Imam

Very briefly, the Imam is the recognized spiritual leader of the masjid. His responsibilities may vary. The training an Imam receives varies from community to community. Some Imams are graduates of prestigious religious Universities that have operated for hundreds of years, such as Al-Azhar in Egypt. At such institutions, an Imam, or interested student (male or female) can obtain certification in a variety of subjects, and earn academic degrees up to the PhD, or equivalent. Also, a person may become an Imam through the tutelage of a learned scholar, or respected learned elder. Imams may be hired by a Board of Directors, or appointed by acclimation of the membership. Many are part-time. Very few to my knowledge earn a living wage as the Imam. Today, several seek employment in hospitals and other healthcare facilities as the Muslim Chaplain.

Although scholarship is open to both men and women, presently, only men are recognized as Imams (organizational leaders) by the community. The Muslim Community follows the revelations of Al-Qur'an as well as the recorded authentic traditions (ahadith) of the Prophet Muhammad (pbuh). There is no tradition of women as Imams (leader of the masjid, or community prayers). However, a woman who leads other women in prayer can be considered the *imam* (leader) in that setting.

Throughout history there have been a number of important women scholars. Nevertheless, men have the final responsibility for leadership of the Muslim Community. In addition to knowledge, there are other criteria for selecting an Imam.

> He who is the most excellent reader of the Holy Qur'an from amongst a party, shall be their Imam. If they are equal in reciting it, he will act as Imam who is the most learned of them in (the knowledge) of Traditions. If they are equal, then he who is the foremost of them in migration, then he who is oldest of them in age. (Shad, 1978, p.10)

There is no hierarchical form of religious governance accepted by most Muslims. For the most part, there is nothing comparable to a pope or General Conference of bishops for oversight. However, there are prestigious universities and respected cultural leaders who maintain regional or national influence in their respective countries. We have not seen this phenomenon develop in in America thus far. Nevertheless, there are a few internationally recognized scholars who have settled in this country.

Traditionally, the Imam performs any or all of the following functions: leads the five daily required prayers; conducts the Friday services *(Jumah)*, as well as the two Eid celebrations (end of Ramadan and end of the Hajj period); performs marriages; presides at the funeral prayer (*janaaz*a); teaches classes in Islamic law (*sharia*); and provides/teaches Qur'anic recitation. In many instances, the Imam is also the administrative head of the masjid. He may function as the chief decision-maker. In other instances, the masjid may have a Board of Directors which may have the authority to hire and fire the Imam.

Sometimes, a community may import an Imam from their cultural homeland, e.g. Pakistan, Mali. The skills that they may bring with them should not be minimized. Nevertheless, the training may not have included analysis of fundamental needs or issues related to the American Muslim experience. For example, Imams need appropriate training, or familiarity in dealing with issues of substance use disorders; mental health challenges; prisoner rehabilitation; family counseling; interfaith work; and financial management. It should be noted that at one time the African American Muslim community had some of these much-needed programs in place (Kepel, 1997, p.33). It is my observation that a crisis of Islamic identity; racism; low communal self-esteem; American racist political pressure; and islamophobia contributed to the depletion of those resources.

In contemporary American society, an Imam finds more and more demands placed upon him. He is expected to fulfill all the religious expectations required of him from his own community. He is expected to respond to media and government inquiries about local and international acts of terrorism. And, he is expected to participate in interfaith activities; especially in the areas of social issues such as health care, homelessness, food security, and police misconduct.

The Imam should be familiar with the basics of Clinical

Pastoral Education (CPE). Furthermore, he should continue his professional education for self-improvement and effectiveness. In regards CPE training, I observed that CPE training can be challenging for imams and other Muslim trainees. I am aware of a dozen Muslims who started the training and did not complete it. Their reasons vary. However, many of them attribute their withdrawal from the programs to their exposure to Christian hegemony, narcissistic personality traits among certain supervisors and colleagues, or patent disregard for anything a Muslims had to say. To a lesser extent, several Rabbis expressed similar concerns. However, they have a longer history of interaction with Christian-dominated CPE programs and appeared to have developed viable coping skills.

Most of the CPE supervisors, interns, and students are Christian. They naturally bring their beliefs, experiences and biases to CPE training; as do we all. Nevertheless, understandably so, much of the literature and many CPE anecdotes draw upon a Christian experience. Christians are comfortable with and incorporate the Hebrew Scriptures into their theology and teaching. This is reflected in CPE training. It appears to me that institutions offering CPE training are not yet ready to include concepts or interpretation from an Islamic religious tradition (or other non-Christian traditions) even though they give lip service to the same.

I observed that even Jewish colleagues still are slighted. They certainly do not need me to defend their position. Nevertheless, here is an example to emphasize my point. To my understanding and observation, most Christian clergy in CPE training are ordained ministers, seminary graduates. They should be well aware of the proper names for the Hebrew Scriptures (Tanakh). The Tanakh is composed of the Torah (five books of Moses), Nevi'im (prophets) and Ketuvim (wittings). Yet in a supposedly culturally competent and open CPE process, supervisors allow the Tanakh to be referred to as *The Old testament*. I do not believe that Jews consider their book an old testament. To my mind, this behavior is inappropriate and insulting. If some Christians behave this way towards their Jewish friends, what can

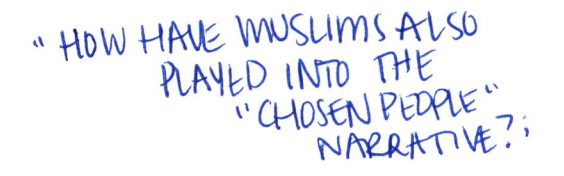

> "HOW HAVE MUSLIMS ALSO PLAYED INTO THE "CHOSEN PEOPLE" NARRATIVE?"

Muslims expect? I have observed similar disrespect directed towards a Yoruba/Lukumi priest and CPE colleague. His religious tradition derives from Africa, the Caribbean, and the South America. Where is the CPE cultural sensitivity/competence? Is there really authentic room for additional religious traditions? It may be time for CPE educators to revisit Jungian concepts of the *shadow self*. I pray that we can reason together and overcome these issues for the sake of the people of G-d.

Chaplaincy, Counseling, and Caregiving

In the religion of Al-Islam, it is a righteous act to attend to the spiritual, emotional and physical needs of a believer. In several revealed verses, this kindness is extended to all of humanity. Al-Qur'an states that people who have good will and perform good deeds will be rewarded many times over for their efforts. Conversely, those who choose a path other than the doing of good, will receive a negative reward comparable to the harm perpetrated. Pastoral care providers, chaplains, counselors, social works and other caregivers may be covered by the spirit of this revelation. Additionally, all efforts are rewarded according to their merit, or lack of merit:

> He that doeth good shall have ten times as much to his credit. He that doeth evil shall only be compensated according to his evil. No wrong shall be done into them. (Al-An'am, 6:160)

Many helping professions concern themselves with the bio-psycho-social-spiritual heath of the individual. Each profession has its own stated objectives. Sometimes these objectives are narrowly focused. Other times, these professions may look for opportunities to expand into new areas of interest (mission creep). The expansion can be the result of meeting new patient needs, or the desire to capture additional funding opportunities. Nevertheless, the overarching intent of these helping professions is to provide a service and *to do no harm* (Hippocratic Oath).

Over the years, there have been some competitive overlap in services provided to clients and hospital patients. Much of this is due to the reduction in funding from federal, state, and local governments. Additionally, funding sources are demanding better and greater professional and cultural competency. One example is in the area of substance abuse counseling. In the States of New York and New Jersey in order to receive a license, now one has to have a Master's Degree in a specific counseling discipline, or equivalent. Additionally, one needs a certain number of required hours of work overseen by a clinical supervision, completion of required coursework, and pass an oral as well as a written test. This standard replaced licensing as a result of completing continuing education units and a significant successful number of years working as a counselor.

      Chaplaincy as a profession has also changed over the years. There was a time when hospitals and nursing homes hired clergy to minister to particular populations. For example, priests ministered to Catholics, and Rabbis to Jews. I have observed that in prison settings, for the most part, this is still the practice. One example is the New York City Department of Corrections (NYCDOC). Imams almost exclusively attend to the Muslim population.

      In the 1990's, I ran into challenges at Riker's Island the first time I went to visit a facility there. At the time, Riker's consisted of 9 facilities for men, and one for women. A detained Christian colleague asked me to make pastoral visits. I requested a visit from the Deputy Warden for Programs. He forwarded my request to the facility's Imam. The Imam informed me that I should not visit the person because Christian clergy visit Christians, and Imams visit Muslims. Nevertheless, after some negotiations, I visited the person on a regular basis. To my knowledge, not much has changed after all these years. Chaplains still visit and minister exclusively to members of their religion/communion

Qur'an and Counseling/Helping Relationship

      To my understanding, there appears to be no direct references in Al-Qur'an to clinical pastoral care, psychology or counseling. Nevertheless, there are references to the human soul and how it can be challenged emotionally and healed. In times of distress, the Muslim is assured that Allah (swt) is always near, for example:

> It was We Who created man, and We know what suggestions his soul makes to him; for We are nearer to him that (his) jugular vein. Behold two (guardians angels) appointed to learn (his doings), learn (and note them). One sitting on the right and one sitting on the left. Not a word does he utter but there is a vigilant Guardian. (Qaf, 50:16-18)

Al-Qur'an suggests that Allah (swt) knows his creation. He decrees and understands the challenges he has given mankind. The actions of men and women are somehow recorded. In modern secular metaphorical terms, we can discuss and compare such recordings to storage devices such as the *computer cloud*, DNA, or flash drives. Qur'anically, our deeds and actions are recorded on our metaphorical hands, feet, hearts, and minds.

> On the Day when their tongues, their hands, and their feet will bear witness against them as to their actions. On that Day Allah will pay them back (all) their just dues, and they will realize that Allah is The (very) Truth, that makes all things manifest. (An-Nur, 24:24-25)

Islamic Compassionate Care, religious advice, as well as caregiving are mercies from Allah (swt). The helping professions are a way to practice charity. Professionals who attend to the physical, mental, social and spiritual needs of individuals obtain special blessings from Allah (swt):

> Believe in Allah and His messenger, and spend (in charity) out of the (substance) whereof He has made you heirs. For, those of you who believe and spend (in charity), for them is a great Reward. (Al-Hadid, 57:7)

Allah (swt) provides a remedy for every disease of mankind. We may not always be aware of remedy. However, Al-Qur'an assures the believer that such a remedy exists. New medical, psychological concepts, and methodologies are discussed and regularly applied in their respective fields by Allah's (swt) Grace. The Prophet Muhammad (pbuh) addressed this concept as follows:

> For every disease, there is a medicine, and if that medicine is applied to the disease, he will recover by Allah's leave. And he said: "Allah has not sent down any disease but He has also sent down the cure; the one who knows it, knows it and the one who does not know it, does not know it." (Bukhari, Vol. 7, Bk.71, No. 582)

Hermeneutics of Suspicion

Al-Quran reminds us that certain degrees of suspicion are a sin. Perhaps, it refers to suspicion based upon irrational fear or bias. Given the recent negative media and political attention given the Muslims community, perhaps some degree of caution, if not suspicion, is appropriate from Muslims. Al-Qur'an also cautions Muslims against spying on each another, and backbiting. These two issues are especially important to Muslims given recent activities of certain federal and local agencies.

> Oh ye who believe! Avoid suspicion as much as possible, for suspicion in some cases is a sin; and spy not on each other, nor speak ill of each other behind their backs. Would any of you like to eat the flesh of his dead brother? Nay, ye would abhor it... but fear Allah, for Allah is Oft-Returning Most Merciful. (Al-Hujurat, 49:12)

Many Muslims carry some degree of *the hermeneutics of suspicion* when interacting with non-Muslim chaplains and CPE educators. By hermeneutics, I refer to the French philosopher Paul Ricoeur who defined hermeneutic in his book on Freud as, *...the theory of the rules that preside over exegesis-that is, over the interpretation of a particular text, or group of signs that may be viewed as a text.* (Ricoeur, 1970, p. 8).

At the core of this suspicion is the concept of exegesis, the interpretation of a particular text. Al-Qur'an, the Hebrew Scriptures, and the New Testament differ significantly on the interpretation of specific revelations. This is especially true in descriptions of the roles of Prophets Muhammad (as), Ibrahim (as), Musa (as), and Isa (as) – blessing be upon them all. Even when Christians mention the word G-d, Muslims may not be certain of the intent or meaning of the specific reference because of varying Christian concepts of the Trinity. Some Christians alternate arbitrarily between reference to *Jesus* and *G-d The Father*. This is especially challenging in mullti-faith events when a prayer is offered and the name of G-d is mentioned.

Trusting Relationship with Christians and Jew

The relationship between American Muslims and the Judeo-Christian community has ranged from cooperative to hostile. African American Muslim challenges included a time when embracing Al-Islam (Nation of Islam, or Sunni tradition) was considered primarily by White Americans, as anti-Christian, anti-Jewish (pro-Palestinian), or Anti-American. One exception to the rule was former world champion Muhammad Ali. Brother Muhammad was at one time despised as a traitor for refusing to be drafted by the military in a war against Vietnam. He openly embraced the Nation of Islam. He became a Muslim Minister appointed by the Honorable Elijah Muhammad. For refusing to be drafted, he was stripped of his heavy-weight crown. Nevertheless, upon his recent death, at his funeral, he was celebrated as a hero of great conscious by a former president, former US Senator, celebrities and thousands of others.

Recently, some Americans appear to be ambivalence or confused concerning their feelings towards immigrant Muslims. On one hand, they express a desire to weave them into the American tapestry. On the other hand, they respond in a xenophobic manner with fear and misunderstanding. The fact that several atrocities here in America have been committed by both American-born and immigrant Muslims has not helped the situation. To add to the mix, Al-Qur'an warns Muslims to be cautious concerning their relationships with Christians and Jews. At the time of the revelation, relations were somewhat strained:

> Oh ye who believe! take not the Jews and the Christians for friends and protectors. They are but friends and protectors of each other. And he amongst you that turns to then (for friendship) is of them. Verily, Allah guideth not a people unjust. (Al-Ma'ida, 5:51)

Al-Qur'an is considered by Muslims to be a fulfillment of the Divine message of prior revelations. Muslims may wonder how it is that Christians and Jews, who are also monotheists, can reject or ignore the revelation:

> Say: Oh people of the book! Do ye disapprove of us for no other reason than that we believe in Allah and the revelations that have come to us and that which came before (us), and (perhaps) that most of you are rebellious and disobedient. (Al-Ma'ida, 5:59)

In Summary, non-Muslim clinicians should be aware that certain historical realities may influence their relationship with some Muslim patients and clients. Indeed, the clinician himself/herself may have to identify and process his/her own traces of Islamophobia (countertransference). It is important to the clinical process to establish *a therapeutic baseline*. Chaplains and other caregivers who do not consider themselves therapists nevertheless also have to establish an *operational baseline* or whatever they choose to call it.

Cultural Competence

Cultural competence is the relatively new trend in health care delivery systems. The objective of cultural competency is to maximize the delivery of services to the client. This is best accomplished by providing services that are responsive to their socio-cultural needs. This means providing information in a language they understand, respecting boundaries, and the like. Agencies in part are responsive to cultural competency because they are driven by the *funding imperative*. The Federal government and many States require a cultural competency component in funding applications. It is defined by the Department of Health and Human Services as follows:

> The term cultural competence means services, supports or other assistance that are conducted or provided in a manner that is responsive to the beliefs, interpersonal styles, attitudes, language and behaviors of individuals who are receiving services, and in a manner that has the greatest likelihood of ensuring their maximum participation in the program. (USDHHS, 2000)

Cultural competency in part is a result of the African Americans civil rights movement. Their former enslavement, protests, suffering, and abuse prompted the 13th Amendment to the US Constitution in 1865. Subsequently, Congress enacted a number of Civil Rights Acts culminating in the Civil Rights Act (CRA) of 1964, as amended. Title VI of the CRA provided that:

> No person in the United States shall, on ground of race, color or national origin, be excluded from participation in, be denied the benefits of, or be subjected to discrimination under any program or activity receiving Federal financial assistance. (US, 1964)

Accordingly, federal agencies promulgated antidiscrimination regulations for states, municipalities, health care agencies, facilities, and other service providers for obtaining funding (US, 2001). Subsequently, states followed suit with similar regulations and Executive orders (NYS, 2011). Based upon US Department of Health and Human Services policies, The Joint Commission (TJC), a certifying organization for health care organizations and programs, sets its own standards for cultural competency (TJC, 3010). As a result of TJC regulations, health care facilities and programs expect that their employees will develop culturally competent skills.

It is possible that clinicians may encounter resistance from older African Americans, including those who are Muslim. They may retain a *collective memory* of institutional abuse by the medical establishment. Some particularly may remember abuses such as the Tuskegee Syphilis Study of the 1970's; that Black incarcerated mothers in South Carolina were used as test subjects in 1996; and experimental abuse of poor Black youth in New York City with the cardiotoxic drug fenfluramine (Washington, 2006). Immigrant American Muslims, especially from the Middle East, also may have feelings concerning drone strikes on their relatives, or rendition practices by the US government. Along with cultural competence should come some degree of political and historical awareness. Several of Carl Rogers' suggestions for being an effective caregiver that can be useful in such cases:

- Be true to yourself
- Permit yourself to understand the other person
- Open channels for authentic communication
- Be accepting of differences/distinctions
- Allow the patient to tell his/or her own story without interference (Rogers, 1961, p. 16-22)

Psychologists and Spiritual Cultural Competency

Chaplains, Counselors and other caregivers may need more than cultural competency training and familiarity in the areas of ethnicity and race. Traditional clinical practices address in one way or another the bio-psycho-social health of a person. This is not enough. In order to be thorough, a clinician must also include some aspect of a *spiritual assessment.* Dr. Viktor Frankl addressed this concern as follows:

> A therapist who ignores man's spiritual side, and is this forced to ignore the will-to-meaning, is giving away one of his most valuable assets. For it is to this will that a psychotherapist should appeal. (Frank, 1986, p. xvi)

Dr. Frankl understood the significance of the incorporating the spiritual side of a person into a mental assessment i.e. a psycho-spiritual assessment. He implied that a clinician should explore this valuable asset. By analogy, the pastoral care specialist should incorporate mental health concerns into his/her practice. Both professionals need to know how to work together and to make *mutual* referrals when appropriate. The well-being of the patient or client should be primary. This and other aspects of *spiritual cultural competency* and should be addressed.

In effect, Dr. Frankl suggested that there is connection between the human spirit and its desire to find meaning. He proposed that mental health strategies may result in impacting, in a healthy way, one's religious concepts or practices. Dr. Frankl alluded to a *healing bridge* between mental health and religion. Dr. Frankl continued by describing a relationship between religion and psychotherapy, and by extension, all helping professions:

> Although religion may not aim at mental health, it might result in it. Psychotherapy, in turn, often results in an analogous by-product; while the doctor is not, and must not be, concerned with the patient to regain his belief in God, time and again this is just what occurs, untended and unexpected as it is. (Gould, 1993, p. 60)

Indeed, a well-trained clinician can help a person cross the bridge as necessary for spiritual well-being. Religion and mental health professionals need not be adversaries. Pastoral caregivers and mental health workers can work as partners for a person's well-being. Clinicians in addition to exploring the spiritual aspects of the patient/client, have the professional responsibility to examine his/her own emotional and spiritual health. Issues of bias, countertransference or self-doubt may not be obvious.

Human Devils

The Islamic concept of human devils is an area where psychotherapists, counselors and Imams can particularly work together. Allah (swt) in His Wisdom permits every kind of human behavior. Al-Qur'an revealed that Allah (swt) created humans in the best mold (At-Tin 95:4-5). He then permitted them free-will to make behavioral choices. These choices operate within the limits of His plan. Some humans behave like saints; others like human devils:

> ...verily, one of you behaves like the people of Paradise... and that which has been written overtakes him and so he behaves like the people of the Hell-fire and then he enters it; and one of you behaves like the people of Hell-fire ...and that which has been written overtakes him and so he behaves like the people of Paradise and then he enters it. (An-Nawawi, Hadith No.4)

As the previous verse stated, there are some people who are destined for Hell. Indeed, they were created for Hell. Only Allah (swt) knows why this is so. This fate awaits both some humans and some the jinn. It may be that for them Hell is a temporary place for cleansing. Allah (swt) is the best Knower:

> Many are the jinns and men We have made for hell. They have hearts wherewith they understand not, eyes wherewith they see not, and ears wherewith they hear not. They are like cattle, - nay more misguided, for they are heedless of warning. (Al-A'raf, 7:179)

Shaytan is charged with seducing humans, assaulting them with his infantry, and sharing wealth and children (Bani Isra-il 17:64). These are just some of the trials. Al-Qur'an reports that only Allah's (swt) Grace can save humans from spiritual assaults and whisperings of Shaytan (An-Nur 24:21). By definition, human devils are people who repeatedly reject faith, whose hearts and hearing are sealed, and whose spiritual eyesight is covered (Al-Baqarah 2:6-7). Indeed, they are mischief makers in the land (Al-Baqarah 2:10-13).

Muslims have to individually make choices. How should one behave? What is the value of righteous behavior? Does it really make a difference? There are people who are destined for the Fire of Hell or the rewards of Paradise. An individual has no way of knowing whether he or she is among them. Or, will he or she be judged according to his/her best deeds. If so, if they fall short of good deeds, can the person depend on Allah's (swt) supplemental Grace? A Muslim you encounter might be emotionally or spiritually conflicted. This might especially be true for Muslims involved in drugs, homosexuality, neglectful of his/her duty to Allah (swt) and Al-Islam, or other questionable behavior. The caregiver should be aware of some of these possible concerns and challenges.

Chapter 3: Al-Islam, Muslims, and American Health Care

...Whosoever removes a worldly grief from a believer, Allah will remove from him one of the griefs on the Day of Judgment. Whosoever alleviates [the lot of] a needy person, Allah will alleviate [his lot] in this world and the next. Whosoever shields a Muslim Allah will shield him in this world and the next. Allah will aid a servant so long as the servant aids his brother.

-Prophet Muhammad (pbuh) - An-Nawawi, Hadith N0. 36

The first thing we can discover about ourselves is that we are always striving towards a goal. We cannot, therefore, imagine the human spirit as a single, static entity. We can best imagine it as a collection of moving parts, developed from a common origin, which strives to achieve a single goal. The teleology, this striving for a goal, is basic to the concept of adaptation, and the life of the psyche is inconceivable without a goal toward which all our efforts redirected.

-Adler. Alfred, Understanding Human Nature p.15.

Introduction

The purpose of this Chapter is to offer a brief discussion on the development of the caregiving professions in America. These professions mainly promote bio-psycho-social-spiritual heath of the individual. Each profession has its stated objectives and focus. Over the years, there have been some competitive overlap in services provided to clients and hospital patients. Chaplains, social workers, psychologist, and counselors may at times compete for the same people; the same dollars. This is most evident in substance use disorder treatment. The profession for the most part is being incorporated into mental health departments/agencies. Former drug treatment organizations appear to be scurrying to become mental health facilities in order to stay relevant. Substance abuse counselors are now seeking certifications which include the provision of mental health services. More and more people with social work degrees have a taken courses in substance abuse and recovery.

The present trend for training chaplains is provided through Clinical Pastoral Education (CPE). Professional standards exist for several somewhat competitive organization. Among these are:

- College of Pastoral Supervision and Psychotherapists (CPSP)
- Association for Clinical Pastoral Education (ACPE), and
- American Association of Pastoral Counselors (AAPC)

The Association of Clinical Pastoral Education, Inc. defines CPE as follows:

> Clinical Pastoral Education is interfaith professional education for ministry. It brings theological students and ministers of all faiths (pastors, priests, rabbis, imams and others) into supervised encounters with persons in crisis. (ACPE, 2016)

I completed four units of CPE. I fulfilled requirements for one unit at Calvary Hospital. Calvary is primarily a Palliative Care/Hospice facility in The Bronx. And, I completed three units in a chaplain residency program at the Episcopal Health Services, St. John's Hospital, Far Rockaway, Queens. I had the opportunity to work with two of the most professional, respected, and brilliant CPE supervisors within the New York City metropolitan area. My foundational religious experience began in the African Methodist Episcopal (AME) Church. At one point in my youth, I was a Sunday school leader for my peer group when the teacher was absent. Additionally, I played piano for the service. Even while studying Al-Islam, I continued to play organ for several Sunday masses at two separate Catholic churches. I was still in my early twenties. For the sake of this discussion, suffice it to say that my quest for a fuller meaning and expression of the oneness of G-d (tawhid) helped me to evolve spiritually. This evolution led me to the religion of Al-Islam.

Given my experiences, I found minimal challenges with the CPE process or with members of my peer groups. As addressed earlier, Carl Rogers' suggestions for being an effective caregiver may be useful to CPE participants, counselors, and other caregivers. I repeat them here for emphasis:

- Be true to yourself
- Permit yourself to understand the other person
- Open channels for authentic communication
- Be accepting of differences/distinctions
- Allow the patient to tell his/or her own story without interference (Rogers, 1961, p.16-22)

It is not clear to me how CPE training will address protocols for mental health encounters. Chaplains have a role to play. Chaplains are not counselors and do not develop time-sensitive treatment plans. Nevertheless, in hospital settings in particular, they may be required to make rounds in detox and/or mental wards. Chaplains should be trained on how to incorporate their spiritual assessments into the overall treatment plan of the healthcare team. If not, in the future they may lose their relevancy, as hospitals consider cutting costs

Psycho-Spiritual Concerns of Contemporary American Muslims
Historic Qur'anic/Biblical Perspective

Muslim patients and clients may well welcome the attention and comfort offered by chaplains and other caregivers. Notwithstanding, there are some historical and phenomenological points that should be mentioned. The following Qur'anic verses can be considered a subtext to relationships between Muslims and Jews/Christians. Caregivers may find the information useful.

Muslims believe that the Prophet Muhammad (pbuh) is the Prophet foretold in the Hebrew Scriptures in Deuteronomy (Davarim). The book speaks of a prophet to come in the future *from among their brethren* (nation of Ishmaelites). This prophet, like Musa (as), was to bring Divine guidance (law). Davarim recorded that The Lord God will put His words in the mouth of this Prophet. Al-Qur'an mentions several Ishmaelite prophets. Most notable Shu'aib (as) (Jethro) the father-on-law of Musa (as), Hud (as) (Eber), and Saalih (as) -peace be upon them all. Only the Prophet Muhammad (pbuh) fulfilled the requirements of Davarim. He received Al-Qur'an in his heart and spoke the words received from Allah (swt). Davsrim recorded this revelation as follows:

> I will raise them up a Prophet from among their brethren, like unto thee, and I will put my words in his mouth; and he shall speak unto them all that I shall command him. And it shall come to pass that whosoever will not harken unto my words which he shall speak in my name, I will require it of him. (Davarim, 18:18-19)

Muslims especially honor the Prophet Ibrahim (as). His position is pivotal in the history of monotheism. We recognize him as a true worshiper of the Allah (swt), The Most High God, and the father of our Prophet Ishmael (as):

> Abraham was not a Jew nor yet a Christian; but he was upright, and bowed his will to Allah's (which is Islam) and he joined not gods with Allah. Without doubt, among men, the nearest of kin

> to Abraham are those who follow him, as are also this Prophet and those who believe; and Allah is the Protector of those who have faith. (Al-Imran, 3:67-68)

The Jew and Christian Scriptures also acknowledge Prophet Ibrahim (as) as a servant of God:

> And Mel-chiz-edek King of Sa'lem, brought forth bread and wine, and he was the Priest of the Most High God. And he blessed him, and said, "Blessed be Abram of the Most High God, which hath delivered thine enemies into thy hand." And he gave him tithes of all. (Beresit, 14:18-19)

According to Jewish and Christian scriptures, Allah (swt) established a sacred covenant between Prophet Ibrahim and his descendants, including Prophet Ismael, his first borne son:

> And I will establish my covenant between me and thee and thy seed after thee in their generations, for an everlasting covenant to be a God unto thee and to thy seed after thee. (Beresit, 17:7)

Muslims claim the historic lineage of the Prophet Ishmael, the son of Prophet Ibrahim (peace be upon both of them). Arab descendants of Prophet Ishmael (as) living in the area of Israel and Palestine believe that they also are of the seed of Prophet Ibrahim (as). This issue may be at the root of present-day conflicts in the Middle East. In effect, the conflict is a *family dispute*:

> And Abram passed through the land unto the place of Si'chem, unto the plain of Mo'reh. And the Ca'naan-ite was then in the land. And the Lord appeared unto Abram and said, "Unto thy seed will I give this land:" and there builded (sic) he an altar unto the Lord, who appeared unto him. (Beresit, 12:6-7)

According to Al-Qur'an, Muslims, Jews and Christians should get along famously in part because they ultimately worship the same Deity and expect fulfillment of a similar promise:

> Those who believe (in the Qur'an), and those follow the

Jewish scriptures, and the Christians and the Sabians, any who believe in Allah and the Last Day, and work righteousness, shall have their reward with their Lord; on them shall be no fear, nor shall they grieve. (Al-Baqarah, 2:62)

Spiritual Roots of Religious Conflict

Historical phenomena and flaws in the human character continue to foment religious conflict. For Muslims, the early challenges faced by the Prophet Muhammad (pbuh) influenced their present view of the world. He was persecuted by his own tribal group, the Quraish. He experienced betrayals by allies. Al-Qur'an warns the vulnerable Muslim community concerning some Jews and Christians. In addition to Al-Ma'ida, 5:51 and 5:59 already cited, the roots of spiritual and religious conflict are discussed as follows:

> Never will the Jews or the Christians be satisfied with thee unless thou follow their form of religion. Say, "The Guidance of Allah, -that is the (only) Guidance." Wert thou to follow their desires after the knowledge which hath reached thee, then wouldst thou find neither Protector nor Helper against Allah. (Al-Baqarah, 2: 120)

and

> They say, "Become Jews or Christians if ye would be guided (to salvation)." Say thou, "Nay! (I would rather) the Religion of Abraham the True, and he joined not gods with Allah." Say ye, "We believe in Allah, and the revelation given to us, and to Abraham, Isma'il, Jacob, and the Tribes, and that given to Moses and Jesus, and that given to (all) Prophets for their Lord. We make no difference between one and another of them; and we submit to Allah." (Al-Baqarah, 2: 135-136)

In their own manner, Jews, Christians, and Muslims are

monotheists and believe in One G-d. They profess to follow the dictates of their respective books. At the root of their beliefs are various intensities of generosity-of-spirit and heart-felt love ordained by their Creator. Nevertheless, competition and mutual rivalry for material things, notions of supremacy, and religious/secular tribalism interfere with their Divine mandates.

All of these factors may influence how some Muslims may feel and respond to Jews and Christians. The challenge for Jewish and Christian caregivers is to be able to develop an authentic therapeutic relationships with their Muslim patients and clients despite any issues of bias or countertransference. The responsibility of the Muslim patient/client is to transcend differences and *to compete with others in the doing of good* (Al-Baqarah, 2:148).

Selected Muslim Psycho-socio-spiritual Concerns

For the sake of this discussion, I will categorize the Muslim population in America into the Indigenous and the Immigrant Muslims. The Indigenous Muslims are part of the African American Community. These are the descendants of formerly enslaved Africans who were forced to migrate to the United States. They are estimated at 42% of the American Muslim population. The remaining 58% of the Muslim population are the immigrant Muslims. These are individuals who freely chose (volunteered) to migrate to America (AMC, 1992, p13). The immigrant Muslims come primarily from Southern Asia, the African peninsula of Arabia, Africa, The Middle East, and Eastern Europe.

Indigenous Muslims share a common history with other African Americans. The history of enslavement of Africans and their descendants is well known and will not be repeated herein. What is less well known or understood is the *collective consciousness* of African American Muslims. I include a brief discussion for informational and clinical purposes.

African American Muslims

Muslims were among the very earliest explorers of the American continent. Their travels are well documented in numerous books, and archives. Muslim explorers arrived here from Africa, e.g., Abu Bakari from the Kingdom of Mali in 1312. Christopher Columbus reported that he saw a masjid near Gibara on the northeast coast of Cuba. And Estevanico who accompanied the Spanish explorer Paniflo de Narva'ez in 1527, was a Muslim from Morocco (Muhammad, 2001, p. 3-5).

Historical records also report that Muslims were among the very first enslaved Africans brought to the Americas. Enslaved Muslims from the Sene-Gambia area of Africa were reported in New York City (1741), Annapolis Maryland (1731), and Norwich Connecticut (1750). Many people are familiar with the story of Alex Haley. He traced his ancestry to Kunte Kinte; his Gambian Muslim ancestor. Early Muslims in America also left a written legacy in Arabic. This included Qur'anic texts, and letters. In some instances, they wrote in Arabic script. However, when vocalized, the words proved to be English (transliterations). It should be remembered that enslaved Africans were considered by the majority of the American population to be uncultured and illiterate. It is significant that some enslaved Muslims were able to read and write.

Muslims have played an important and active role in the history of America. The word *maroons* described enslaved Africans who escaped from the horrors of plantation life. Scholars believe this word had its origin in the word *Moors*, another word for Muslim Africans. Some historians believe that some present-day Native Americans are possible descendants of early Muslims. These peoples/tribal nations may include the Alibamu of Alabama, Apaches, Black Indians of the Schuylkill river area in New York, Seminoles, and others. Historically, it is documented that several Native Americans Nations accepted escaping Africans including Muslims into their communities. And, a Muslim named Mohammed Ali ben Said (1822-1882), also known as Nicolas Said, joined the 55th Regiment of Massachusetts Colored

Volunteers in the Civil War. He became a sergeant in 1863 (Muhammad, 2001, p. 15-30).

The social and political history of African Americans also contributed to the development of their collective conscious. American racial attitudes concerning slavery played a large part in the mental health of African Americans. Colonial enslavement was the law of the day. Later, Africans were considered to be less than human, and unfit to interact on a personal level with White Americans. This political sentiment was expressed by Justice Taney in his deliberation during the Dred Scott case of 1854:

> They [the Negroes] had for more than a century before been regarded as beings of an inferior order, and altogether unfit to associate with the white race, either in social or political relations; and so far inferior, that they had no rights which the white man was bound to respect. (US. 1856)

Indeed, enslavement was viewed as a natural state for Africans in America. Opposition or resistance constituted a mental disorder. Dr. Samuel Cartwright, a noted Louisiana physician discussed this notion in a 1851 article. He identified two diseases prone to enslaved Africans. The first was *drapetomania*. This alleged disease caused enslaved Africans to flee the plantation for freedom in the North. His second discovery was *dysaesthesia aethiopica*. It allegedly caused enslaved Africans to do the following:

> … cut up corn, cane, cotton or tobacco when hoeing it, as if for pure mischief. They raise disturbances with their overseers and fellow-servants without cause or motive, and seem to be insensible to pain when subjected to punishment. It is much more prevalent among free negroes living in clusters by themselves, than among slaves on our plantations, and attacks only such slaves as live like free negroes in regard to diet, drinks, exercise, etc. It is not my purpose to treat of the complaint as it prevails among free negroes, nearly all of whom are more or less afflicted with it, that have not got some white

person to direct and to take care of them. (Cartwright, 1851)

Enslaved Africans and their descendants were emancipated by the 13th Amendment to the Constitution of the United States. It was ratified in 1865. Nevertheless, racist ideology and practice continued in the medical field. Census records between 1860 and 1890 showed that insanity among the Africans and their descendants, practically unheard of before 1890, increased from 1 in 10,584 to 1 in 943 (approximately 10 times). Dr. T. O. Powell, superintendent of the Georgia Lunatic Asylum, attributed the increase to emancipation. Dr. Powell suggested that *freedom* made Africans and their descendants crazy:

> Freedom, however, removed all hygienic restraints, and they were no longer obedient to the inexorable laws of health, plunging into all sorts of excesses and vices, leading irregular lives, and have apparent little or no control over their appetites and passions. (Jackson, n.d.).

Throughout the history of American medicine and mental health practices, enslaved and formerly enslaved Africans and their descendants were used as subjects for dangerous radical surgery. They were inoculated with smallpox and other agents. They were used to test vaccines and subsequently and possibly permitted to die so that their bodies could be used for dissection, or for medical schools, and/or experimented upon in prisons (Jackson, n.d.)

Some of the early self-help efforts to address the psychological condition of African Americans are found among the Muslims. One of the strategies was to reclaim the religion of Al-Islam which was stripped from enslaved Africans. One of the pioneers in this effort was The Honorable Noble Drew Ali (1886-1929). He viewed Al-Islam as a form of *liberation theology*. In 1913, he established The Moorish Science Temple (MST). Moor was another term for Muslim. He taught that African Americans were Asiatics, not Negroes or Blacks. He also taught that the historical home of the members of the MST was the Kingdom of Morocco.

The Moorish Science Temple offered Islam as a religious ideology for combating the psychological and emotional effect of the post-enslavement period. His organization offered the beginnings of Islamic Compassionate Care and Counseling. The principles of the organization included:

- Teach the "Koran,"
- Teach, preach, and live the religion of Islam,
- Establish the faith of Islam in America., and
- Reclaim Islamic family names such as *Ali, El,* and *Bey* (FBI, 1942)

The men of the Temple wore a red Moroccan-style fez and a beard. The membership card was decorated with a star and crescent. It also contained a statement that the person was *a Moslem under the Divine Laws of the Holy Koran of Mecca, Love, Truth, Peace, Freedom, and Justice.* It ended with a statement that the person *was a citizen of the United States* (Kepel, 1997. P.21). This was an effort to regain and improve self-esteem among the African American. The Honorable Noble Drew Ali predated The Honorable Elijah Muhammad (1897-1975).

The Honorable Elijah Muhammad is generally considered to be one of the founders of the Nation of Islam. There is some controversy concerning this teachings. However, for the purpose of this discussion, he is important for several reasons:

- He was a pioneer of Islamic discourse in America,
- He discussed African American/African American Muslim issues of theology, social psychology, self-esteem, self-determination and self-development.
- He established the religious framework for intellectual curiosity that inspired generations of African Americans

through concepts of *the original man, know thyself,* and *do for self.* (Muhammad, 1965, p,56)

The Honorable Elijah Muhammad evolved as a great leader and social psychologist for African American Muslims. He advanced a worship system that accentuated positive and healthy behaviors for developing attitudes of self-worth, knowledge of self, and self-development. He directed his philosophy and actions towards the betterment of the African American people in general (business development, healthy diet). His directives for the Nation of Islam (NOI) included ritual prayer, clean living, and development of family values.

He saw the religion of Islam as a cure for the ills and self-hatred exhibited by African Americans. Bernard Chushmeer, in his book *This is the One*, summarized the efforts of the Honorable Elijah Muhammad as follows:

> His is the hardest job any man has ever had. He has the staggering task of giving mental (spiritual) life to the dead (Black people). Despite opposition from every direction, he is unifying the most divided people on earth. He is raising a people who were deprived of the very base of self-respect and dignity. That base is the knowledge of self and others. (Chushmeer, 1971, p.8)

The Honorable Elijah Muhammad understood and promoted education as a tool for liberating the minds of African Americans.

> Elijah Muhammad concerned himself with specific purposes of education. For Muhammad, the purpose of education was a very straight-forward one: To develop the minds of the Negro, and to advance the welfare of his people. In doing this, the practical aspects of the Negro's life were to be turned into self-fulfillment, as enhanced through economic self-reliance. From a base of economic self-reliance, other values and self-determination would come. Self-education, therefore, had a utilitarian purpose. (Alexander, 1981, p. 88)

Reverend Dr. James H. Cone explained that African American culture should be used in a *liberation theology of the oppressed*. He posited that this theology would give more meaning to the Christian experience for African Americans. There are some African American Muslims who view the religion of Al-Islam as liberation theology. They posit that African America Muslim culture may well adapt itself to give more meaning to an American Islamic approach to theology.

On the death of The Honorable Elijah Muhammad in 1975, his son Imam Warith Deen Muhammad assumed the leadership of the Nation of Islam. He altered some of the basic principles of his father and brought the organization more in line with traditional practices of Muslims Worldwide. He changed the name of the organization several times, finally settling on the *American Society of Muslims*. Imam Muhammad also promoted a business self-development model for his community. Some members objected to Imam Muhammad's direction and reestablished the philosophical principles of The Honorable Elijah Muhammad.

The Honorable Silas Muhammad was the first to object. Shortly after the death of The Honorable Elijah Muhammad, he reestablished the *Lost-Found Nation of Islam (NOI)*. He also obtained control of the legal name and publication of the organization newspaper *Muhammad Speaks*. Minister Muhammad went back to the original principles of the NOI as stated on the last pages of the *Muhammad Speaks* newspaper. Also Mr. Muhammad is a noted human rights advocate. He submitted a petition on the human rights of African Americans for recognition as a *national minority* under appropriate United Nations resolutions and Covenants. Specifically, he wrote to Boutros Boutros-Ghali, former secretary General of the UN in March 1994 requesting the same (NOI,1994).

The Honorable Luis Farrakhan, a Minister under The Honorable Elijah Muhammad, also left Imam Warith Deen's organization. In 1979, he founded *The Final Call*. I believe that this was the name originally for both his organization as well as the newspaper he established. The newspaper followed the same tradition as the original *Muhammad Speaks* newspaper. They both contained similar language on what Muslims believe and what they want:

> WE BELIEVE that Allah (God) appeared in the Person of Master W. Fard Muhammad, July, 1930; the long-awaited "Messiah" of the Christians and the "Mahdi" of the Muslims. We believe further and lastly that Allah is God and besides HIM there is no god and He will bring about a universal
> government of peace wherein we all can live in peace together. (NOI, 2014)

Minster Farrakhan is noted for his international work for world peace among African nations. In 1988, he purchased the former flagship NOI masjid in Chicago. In 1995, he coordinated and led the *Million Man March on Washington, D.C.* The march attracted nearly two million African American men. The objective of the march focused on spiritual healing of Black men needed as a result of concern for negative images perpetuated by the media and movie industries. Also, he addressed substance use disorders and recovery; as well as gang violence in our communities.

African American Muslims share historical experiences with African Americans. I already mentioned some of the socio-theological challenges experienced within the community. Some African American Muslims embraced Al-Islam for its theological values. Others may have join for its religious discipline, Islamic cultural restrictions on some behaviors, and emphasis on family and community. An understanding or review of these conditions may assist in clinical assessments and caregiving. The remaining discussion applies primarily to the psycho-social challenges to the African American Muslim Community as a part of the larger African American population.

I observe that issues of skin color, hair texture and clothing trends still have their effects on the African American Community at large. Additionally, the community faces issues of racism, poverty, underemployment, and predator economics. These concerns may have severe psychological and emotional impacts on individuals. I cannot adequately address these subjects in this work. However, I offer a few comments for their contextual probative value in caregiving. Many of these issues remain *shadow remnants* in the African American unconscious. African American Muslims share these concerns. However, embracing Al-Islam adds a particular dynamic. It appears acceptable for an African American to embrace Christianity. There are even African Americans who have been accepted into various Jewish traditions. Nevertheless, outside of family members and *the hood*, many African American Muslims experience varying degrees suspicion or emotional distance from the larger society. A brief history of common African American psycho-social challenges may be instructive and helpful.

As late as the 1930's, African Americans, were still challenged by the psychological pressures of the dominant American culture. Dr. Kenneth Clark presented research in 1939 that indicated degrees of self-hatred among African American youth. When given the choice, young girls chose white dolls over black dolls, in part because of the prevailing, Caucasian standards of beauty, and the overwhelming dominance of white culture. Dr. Clark noted:

> It is clear that the Negro child by the age of five is aware of the fact that to be colored in contemporary American society is a mark of inferior status. (Clark, 1950, p.34-35)

In more recent times, African Americans have made efforts to combat the onslaught of negative psychological attitudes, and questionable medical/mental health practices in our communities. In the area of educational counseling, Mr. Jawanza Kunjufu developed concepts to reverse the school drop-out rate, and disturbing lack of interest in education among young Black men. In the Introduction to Mr. Kunufu's book, Useni Eugene Perkins discussed its importance of addressing the education of our youth:

> Brother Jawanza chooses to concentrate on the destruction of African American boys, because he feels that the African-

American male poses the greatest threat to white supremacy. For it is during their childhood that the system of American racism and oppression begins to cripple African American males, so that when they reach adulthood, they are socially, physically, and politically impotent. (Kunjufu, 1985, p. vii)

In further discussion about African American self-images, Dr. Alvin Poussaint, a psychiatrist, described the basis for the undesirable physical image of young Black children. Black psychiatrists like Dr. Alvin Poussaint and Dr. Frances Cress Welsing have spoken out about their own challenges with White psychiatrists and social workers and their racist perceptions of African Americans (Poussaint, 1972, p. 26) and (Welsing, 1991, p, xi). In reference to the self-image of Black children, Dr. Poussaint stated the following:

Black children, like all children, come into the world victims of factors over which they have no control. In the looking glass of white society, the supposedly undesirable physical image of "Tar Baby" -- black skin, wooly hair and thick lips is contrasted unfavorably with the valued model of "Snow White," -- white skin, straight hair and aquiline features. (Poussaint, 1974, p16)

Today there is an effort among African American psychologists to balance their desire to meet the mental health need of their community, and at the same time, address the racists and oppressive cultural practices that still exist in varying degrees in the counseling, psychological, and psychiatric professions. The notion of good health is best established by that which is *normal*. Normality in America is based upon the values of the white American middle class. Dr. Na'im Akbar discusses the short-fall of this standard as follows:

From the Eurocentric reference point, normality is established on a model of the middle class, Caucasian male of European descent. The more one approximates the model in appearance, values and behaviors, the more "normal" a person is considered to be. The major problem with such normative assumptions for non-European people is the inevitable conclusion of deviance on the part of anyone unlike the model. (Akbar, 2004, p.37)

I caution caregivers to especially be aware or their message to Muslim patients and clients. Please be mindful that a Muslim client may respond to your affect, body language, or air of superiority. Some of your behaviors may be unconscious. Black Psychology evolved to address these Eurocentric attitudes. Dr. Ni'am Akbar discussed its value and contribution to the profession:

> Black Psychology emerged from the kind of negative evaluation of African Americans that have characterized the vast majority of the European American psychology literature. Black Psychology was a reaction. It remains the political or militant arm of the study of African Americans within the European American context. Black Psychology is self-affirmative, particularly in its denial of the denigrating conceptualizations of European American psychology. (Akbar, 2004, p.37)

Some Black mental health scholars still believe that the issues of former enslavement of African Americans had not been adequately addressed. Dr. Joy Degruy Leary is such as person. Her contention is that there is a condition she called the *Post Traumatic Slave Syndrome (PTSS)*. It is a condition that exists as a consequence of multi-generational oppression of Africans and their descendants, resulting from centuries of chattel slavery. (Leary, 2006)

African American Muslims claim their Islamic as well as their African American *heritage* (cultural values) as previously mentioned. Nevertheless, we acknowledge that our *history* here has been a challenging experience. We emphasize our past enslavement experience in America as a part of our history, not a part of our *heritage* (inheritance). Our experiences underscore the need for Islamic compassionate care from our Muslims leaders and appropriate compassionate care for our non-Muslims colleagues. Without this care, African Americans/African American Muslims may continue to be the victim of the *shadows* of:

- Post Traumatic Slavery Syndrome
- Institutional Racism
- Medical Malpractice and,
- Psychological warfare.

In summary, African American indigenous Muslims are the descendants of formerly enslaved Africans. Many of our descendants have reclaimed the Religion of Al-Islam. Some have adopted or integrated the flavor of one or another of the immigrant Muslim cultures. Others are content to forge a truly African American Muslim path. African American Muslims carry a double challenge. They are Muslims, and African Americans. Their bio-psycho-socio-spiritual journey in America has been, and continues to be, challenged at the individual and collective levels. Nevertheless, because of their particular American historical perspective and experience, they lead the dialogue on the meaning of being Muslim and American in the 21st century. Those caregivers and educators best equipped with knowledge of the African American Muslim experience can be able to better apply their clinical skills effectively and serve this community.

Immigrant Muslims

The statistics concerning the number of immigrant Muslims as a part of the Muslim population in the US varies greatly. As stated earlier, The American Muslim Council in 1992 suggested that in the United States the African American Muslims were the largest population at 42%, followed by South Asians 24%, Arabs 12.4%, Africans 5.2%, and others 16.4% (Nu'man, 1992, p.13). There are an estimated 1,209 masjids in the US (Bagby, et al, 2001) and about 70 masjids in NYC (NYT, 1993). There is not reliable data on today's NYC masjids. There are anecdotal estimates of more than 200.

According to the above static, Arabs represent only 12.4% of the American Muslim population. Nevertheless, they appear to hold a place of significance among some Muslims. This may be true even when some non-Arab Muslims have issues with the attitudes of certain Arabs. This may be related in part to the air of superiority expressed by certain Arabs ostensibly because:

- The birthplace of the Prophet Muhammad (pbuh) and other certain scared historic sites are under Arab control (Saudi Arabia)
- Al-Qur'an was revealed in an ancient Arab dialect
- The ahadith and certain historical documents are written Arabic
- Arabs were the first to carry the message Al-Islam to other peoples, and
- For years, popular culture portrayed an Arab as *the Muslim icon.*

Some of the immigrants who come from Arabic-speaking countries do not claim Arab ethnicity, e.g. Kurds and Berbers. There are significant populations of Arab non-Muslims in Arab countries such as Orthodox Christians and Jews. In the US, the largest population of immigrant Muslims comes from Pakistan and India (24%). Even though the Arab population is less than half (12%) of the American Muslim population, the archetype Muslim in the American subconscious appears to be the Arab. Historically, the American media (movies, television, and romantic novels) have contributed to this phenomenon.

Muslim Immigrant can be defined as those who voluntarily left their countries of origin, for whatever reason or conditions, and freely migrated to the United States. Sometimes, immigrants leave for economic consideration. In other instances, they leave to avoid persecution in their native countries. Many Muslim immigrants who come to America are highly trained academically or professionally, and often financially stable. They can be observed in major hospitals as surgeons and administrators, or in industry and government as engineers and scientists. In any event, their intentions for immigrating were very personal. It is my observation, not necessarily a criticism, that for the most part, Muslim immigrants do not come to the US in the interest of the religion of Al-Islam. Comparable to other immigrants, they come for the *American dream.*

In Al-Islam, the intention of a person is significant. Though intention implies a cognitive process, it can also suggest feeling in the heart (affect). Indeed, there is a hadith that confirms this notion. It says that a person achieves that which he/she intends. The hadith is as follows:

> Actions are but by intention, and every man shall have but that which he intended. Thus, he whose migration was for Allah and His messenger, his migration was for Allah and His messenger; and he whose migration was to achieve some worldly benefit, or to take some woman in marriage, his migration was for that for which he migrated. (An-Nawawi, Hadith 1)

It is generally agreed that the first wave of Muslim immigrants arrived about the year 1875. They came mainly from the areas that are today Syria, Lebanon, and Palestine for economic and/or political reasons. They settled in lower Manhattan, and in various parts of Brooklyn. During the beginning of the 20th century, Muslims immigrated to the USA from additional countries, and established masjids:

- Polish Tartars established *The American Mohammed Society* in Brooklyn (1907)
- Albanian Muslims established a masjid in Biddeford, Maine (1915), and in Connecticut (1919)
- Dr. Mufti Muhammad Sadiq established the headquarters of the Ahmadiyya Muslim community in Chicago (1921). For many years, the Ahmadiyya community had a close working relationship with the African American

community. They were the first Muslim immigrants to reach out actively to the African American Muslim community.
- Islamic Center of Washington, DC (1957). President Eisenhower gave the opening remarks. (Muhammad, 2001, p. 53-56)

Other significant immigrant developments included the founding of the Islamic Circle of North America (ICNA), a predominately Indo-Pakistani organization; and the Islamic Society of North America (ISNA), a predominately Arab organization.

In the past, in their attempt to integrate into the American society, many immigrant Muslims either shortened their names or Anglicized them. For instance, some allowed themselves to be called *Mo*, as a nickname for Muhammad, or Al, a shortened form of Ali. When I asked the reason for this behavior, several suggested that their own names were too difficult to pronounce, or sounded too foreign. I found this somewhat amusing considering that there are many Welsh and Eastern European names with challenging spellings and pronunciations. For me, this apparent *denial* of their Muslim names implied feeling of guilt and shame.

The initial days and months after the World Trade Center disaster were unpredictable and dangerous for Muslims, especially in the New York Metropolitan area. After the events of September 11, 2001, both African American and Immigrant Muslims were the subject of religious/cultural backlashes. Many immigrant Muslims kept a low-profile. This was understandable considering that some men and women wear culturally identifiable clothing such as head coverings (hijabs) or an ankle-length one –piece covering (galabia). Even years afterwards, Muslims are still being attacked (Stack, 2016).

Due to harassment, immediately after 9/11, the Imam at the Islamic Center of New York, the City's flagship masjid, abruptly left the City and returned to Egypt. Many business men closed their facilities in fear; and families were split apart as a result of federal government extra-judicial detentions. Others suffered traumatic emotional distress; and undercover policeman and government agencies spied on, or infiltrated community masjids (AP, 2006). Several of the more popular Imams engaged in defensive and protective media strategies with interfaith colleagues. The apparent objective was to explain that they and their respective communities were *the right kind of Muslims*.

However, in recent times, I observe that many youth are less concerned with denying who they are as Muslims. They have normalized their American experience. This is especially true for 2nd generation immigrants. They appear to have strong ego strength and self-determination. For example, more young women wear a head-covering (hijab). Men and woman participate more fully in business, media, and sports without fear of being rejected or ostracized. Muslim youth appear to have a clearer understanding of historic civil and human rights issues in the US. They demonstrate improved relationship with younger imams and other ethnic Muslims; especially on college campuses. Nevertheless, young Muslims are not exempted from the social ills affecting youth in general; including substance use disorders and mental health issues.

Summary

The African American Muslim Community has its own psycho-socio-spiritual challenges. It has an Islamic heritage, yet a history of enslavement in the US. According to the late Dr. Yusuf Naim Kly (Kly,1990), an African American Muslim and professor of political science, the United States consists historically of three groups of people: the Indian Nations (Native Americans), the Settler Nation (Europeans), and those who were enslaved and forced to migrate to America (African Americans). Historically, Settler Nations subjugated the indigenous people(s), created laws, and a ratified a constitution (social contract). That was precisely the sequence of political events which occurred here in the USA. Dr. Kly suggested that, while the English Settler's social contract (the US Constitution) governed their activities, there also existed, in fact, an *Anti-Social Contract* (negative administrative philosophy/government activities). Accordingly, this form of unwritten social contract was intended for enslaved Africans and Native Americans. (Kly, 1989, p.2) By extension, the concept of an Antisocial Contract can be applied today to non-European immigrants, including Muslims. Perhaps, social controversy resulting from the 2016 Presidential election will bring this topic to light again. The election appears to be a clarion call by White America to revisit their notion of historic entitlement in order to *make America great again*.

Immigrant Muslims have appealed to the American ideal of multiculturalism as an answer to their situation. In Imam Dr. Ahmed Kobeisy's book entitled *Counseling American Muslims*, he addressed the issues of American Muslims immigrants in particular:

> Despite this tremendous growth, the Muslim community continues to be unstudied, widely misunderstood, and falsely stereotyped. Research and studies pertaining to Muslim populations with respect to counseling and other mental health fields is at best minimal, and in most cases superficial and judgmental. Most of the few studies made on Muslims in mental health issues are based mainly on religious textual information that describes religious ideals and cultural norms, rather than considering empirical data that indicate individual differences and social factors. (Kobeisy, 2004, p.1)

The World Trade Center disaster and subsequent backlash have challenged the Muslim Immigrant Community in ways that still have repercussions a decade and a half later. Over the years, African American Muslims and Immigrant Muslims have had friendly and not so friendly relationships. In the past, many Muslim immigrant voted primarily Republican. We observed this in the New York City Metropolitan Area. Large numbers of the immigrants voted in the Mayoral elections for Rudolf Giuliani, and in the national election for George W. Bush. This caused a major split, politically and emotionally, with the African American Muslim Community for several years.

However, after the attack on the World Trade Center on September 11, 2001, and in the wake of the subsequent polices of the Bush administration, the relationship improved. This positive relationship may continue to improve given the uncertainty of the social and immigration policies of a Donald J. Trump admiration. It is my prayer that this brief discussion on the historic realities of American Muslims will greatly add to the clinical tools and understanding of caregivers to Muslim and non-Muslims alike.

Chapter 4: The Culture/Tradition of the Muslim Family

> *Men are the protectors and maintainers of women because Allah has given the one more (strength) than the other and because they support them from their means. Therefore, the righteous women are devoutly obedient, and guard in (the husband's) absence what Allah would have them guard.*
>
> **-An-Nisaa 4:34**

> *The human compulsion towards community and communal life is revealed in institutions whose forms we do not need to understand fully; for example, in religion where group worship creates a bond between members of the congregation...The need for community governs all human relationships. Communal life predates the individual life of humanity. In the history of human civilization, no way of life has emerged of which foundations were not laid communally; human beings developed not singly but in communities.*
>
> **-Adler. Alfred, Understanding Human Nature, p.22**

The Family in Al-Islam

The concept and role of family is fundamental within the religion of Al-Islam. Al-Qur'an describes specific guidance for protection, maintenance, interaction, responsibility, and accountability of the family and its members. Al-Qur'an clearly defines the functional roles of men and women. Generally speaking, men and women are physically different. Some even say that they are emotionally different. Al-Qur'an is silent on any emotional distinctions. Nevertheless, these facts sometimes lead to specific areas of comparative advantages between the two. Observably, men demonstrate greater physical strength and are more war-like (protective). Notwithstanding contemporary Western political and cultural values, women are physically designed for child-bearing and are generally observed demonstrating a more family-nurturing disposition/role. These advantages, from ancient times, have ensured the continued existence, development and protection of the human species. Al-Qur'an assigns men the role of protector. He also is responsible for maintaining and supporting the family.

Al-Qur'an states that Allah (swt) created men and women. This basic family unit consists of a husband, wife, and off-spring. He also divided humanity into blood-grouping (clans), family grouping (tribes), and tribal groupings (nations). The survival of these groupings depended on cooperation, loyalty, and sharing in some form of economics/economy. It is the sense of the *common good* and various social restrictions (laws/taboos) that helped to ensure the success of various human societies. Al-Qur'an addresses this concept as follows:

> Oh mankind! We created you from a single (pair) of a male and a female, and made you into nations and tribes, that ye may know each other (not that ye may despise each other). Verily the most honored of you in the sight of Allah is (he who is) the most righteous of you. And Allah has full knowledge and is well acquainted (with all things). (Al-Hujurat, 49:13)

It is clear that differences and distinctions among humans are normal. Our differences allow us to appreciate, compare, and contrast various subtleties in appearances, concepts, and behaviors. According to the revelation, Allah (swt) observes our individual and collective behaviors and our sense of righteousness. Al-Qur'an defines righteousness as follows:

> It is not righteousness that you turn your faces towards East or the West, but it is righteousness to believe in Allah and the last day, and the angels and the Book, and the messengers; to spend of your substance, out of love for Him for your kin, for the orphans, for the needy, for the wayfarer, for those who ask, and for the ransom slaves, to be steadfast in prayer, and give Zakaat; to fulfill the contacts which ye have made, and to be firm and patient, in pain (or suffering) and adversity, and throughout all periods of panic. Such are the people of truth, the God-fearing. (Al-Baqarah, 2:177)

Traditions may vary from social group to social group. Taboos such as incest, adultery, or homosexuality may be imposed to protect the long-range stability of the clan/nation. Cheikh Anata Diop, the Senegalese historian, physicist, and anthropologist, addressed basic societal and familial interactions as follow:

> Clanic organizations, in that it is founded on the taboo of incest, marks the beginning of civilization: the human being is no longer a simply biological animal. His sexual relationships are henceforth dependent on very strict social regulations. The clan is also and above all a social organization whose purpose is to meet economic needs and to challenge nature. It is founded on a deliberate choice of a unilateral type of kinship (patrilineal or matrilineal, according to the economic context), of private or collective type of ownership, of a mode of inheritance, etc. (Diop, 1991, p. 111)

Al-Qur'an describes certain inalienable rights and responsibilities of family members in particular, and the khalifah

(Muslim society) in general. These rights and responsibilities pertain to family, and others:

> Serve Allah, and join not any partners with Him; and do good-to parents, kinsfolk, orphans, those in need, neighbors who are kin, neighbors who are strangers, the companion by your side, the way-farer (ye meet), and what your right hand possess for Allah loveth not the arrogant, the vainglorious. (An-Nisaa, 4:36, p.221)

Parents, mothers in particular, require particular consideration. Parents provide protection and sustenance for themselves and their families. Parents should be respected even in their old age:

> And We have enjoined on man (to be good) to his parents; in travail did his mother bear him and in years twain was his weaning. (Hear the command) "Show gratitude to Me and to thy parents; to Me is (thy final) Goal." (Luqman, 31:14)

and

> Their Lord hath decreed that ye worship none but Him, and that ye be kind to parents, whether one or both of them attain old age in thy life. Say not to them a word of contempt, nor repel them, but address them, in terms of honor; and out of kindness, lower to them the wing of humility, and say, "My Lord! bestow on them Thy mercy even as they cherished me in childhood." (Bani Isra-il, 17: 23-24)

The Prophet Muhammad (pbuh) discussed the primacy of the relationship to one's mother in several hadiths. In several traditions, repeating a sentence or phrase denotes the importance of the statement. In the following hadith, the role of the mother is recognized to be three time deserving of more respect than the father in certain respects:

> Someone asked the Prophet, "Who deserves my service most after Allah?" The Prophet said, "Your mother." The person asked again, "And who is next?" The Prophet said, "Your

mother." The man asked further, "And who is next?" The Prophet replied, "Your mother." The man asked once more, "And who is next?" The Prophet, peace be upon him, said, "Your father." (Yazid, 1953, 17).

and

Paradise is under the feet of the mothers. (Abu Abd al-Rahman, 1930, p.17)

Al-Qur'an contains many examples of Allah's (swt) guidance and pronouncements on gender equity. In terms of adherence to Allah's (swt) guidance, men are not better than or more accountable than women. Each will be rewarded or punished according to his/her actions:

Whoever works righteousness, man or woman, and has faith, verily to him (or her) will We give a life that is good and pure, and We will bestow on such their reward according to the best of their actions. (An-Nahl, 16:97)

Examples of Specific Equal Treatment Between Men and Women

I have observed that equality for the most is a mental construct. It appears most often in mathematics with the use of *equal signs*. Ontologically, things are different and distinct. Qur'anicly, Allah (swt) created distinctions and differences between men and women, the sun and the moon, and day and night for His own purposes. It is a human trait to contrast and compare. We rank and rate various qualities applying those skills.

The major concern in human relationships should be on *fair treatment*. Fair treatment implies the distribution of resources according to established needs and the wellness of the family. Men, women, and children have their individual needs within the family. The family should work together for its own wellbeing. Al-Qur'an gives us guidance for fair treatment:

And in no wise covet those things in which Allah hath bestowed His gifts more freely on some of you than on

> others; to men is allotted what they earn, and to women what they earn; but ask Allah of His bounty for Allah hath full knowledge of all things. (An-Nisaa, 4:32)

Al-Qur'an has a chapter entitled An-Nisaa (The Women). It is chapter number four (4). Verses 1-14 discuss mutual rights of men and women; protecting/restoring the rights of inheritance of property for siblings and orphans as they become of age; dowries for women upon marriage; and punishment in the *hell fire* for violators. And, verses 15-42 provide Allah's (swt) guidance regarding marital relationships, divorce/disputes, and social infractions.

Women should be treated with kindness. Their desires/wills must be respected. Even when men have issues or disputes with their wives, men are encouraged to work-through their domestic challenges. Deception and/or scheming against women is discouraged. Al-Qur'an suggests that there may be innate good lodged in the challenges within marital relationships:

> Oh ye who believe!, ye are forbidden to inherit women against their will; nor should ye treat them with harshness, that ye may take away part of the dower ye have given them;- except, where they have been guilty of open lewdness. On the contrary, live with them on a footing of kindness and equity; if ye take a dislike to them, it may be that ye dislike a thing, and Allah brings about through it a great deal of good. (An-Nisaa, 4:19)

When married couples have agreed on a divorce, a waiting period called a *iddat* is required. During this period, the couple can reconcile or agree to definitely terminate the marriage. Al-Qur'an warns men against taking unfair advantage of, or abuse these delicate situations.

> When ye divorce women, and they (are about to) fulfil the terms of their 'iddat, either take them back on equitable terms, or set them free on equitable terms; but do not take them back to injure them, or to take undue advantage. If

anyone does that, he wrongs his own soul. Do not treat Allah's signs as a jest; but solemnly rehearse Allah's favor on you, and the fact that He sent down to you The Book of Wisdom for your instruction; and fear Allah, and know that Allah is well acquainted with all things. (Al-Baqarah, 2:231)

The Divine Revelation and Rationale Concerning Polygamy

One of the most controversial issues for Westerners is the concept and practice of polygamy. Polygamy among Muslims has historical and phenomenological origins. The institution of polygamy was a practical solution to an existential situation; i.e. the loss of males during defensive wars. Since men still find opportunities to kill one another, decimate their numbers, create widows, and reduce the number of mates for unmarried women, the concept of polygamy may still be a valid option. There are strict guidelines that must be followed. As with any guidance, rules/laws are only as relevant as the power of the authorities designated to enforce them.

For various reasons still being debated and not herein explored, incest and marriage by close relatives historically was prohibited. People formed extended families with neighboring clans. Intermingling and exogamy cemented social relations for common protection and development. Dr. Diop discussed this phenomenon as follows:

> The passage from clan to monolingual tribe, i.e. to ethnic group, to nation, is a consequence of clan exogamy; biological and material reasons, the nature of which is still being discussed by specialist, very early led to archaic society to practice the prohibition of incest, which marked the starting point of civilization. Clan endogamy being prohibited, several neighboring clans contracted marriage ties that with the time became bonds of kinship alliance. (Diop, 1991, p. 116)

Kinship alliances imply that the family/clan will provide for and protect it members. Men usually start and fight wars. It is inevitable that some will be killed. This can leave a society with a significant number of widows and orphans. It is an Islamic belief that widows and marriageable female orphans should not be left unprotected by society. They should have the opportunity to become a part of a family. Alternative choices may lead them to adultery, prostitution, thievery, or some other serious social offense. Certain offenses carried the death penalty. In any event, the society had the responsibility to address its particular needs.

The revelation for multiple marriage appeared in reference to the result of the battle of Uhud. After this battle, the fledgling Muslim community found itself with many female orphans, widows and war captives. These people had to be incorporated into the community. Men were permitted to marry up to four wives. This assumed that they could provide equitably for each of them.

> To orphans restore their property (when they reach their age). Nor substitute (your) worthless things for (their) good ones; and devour not their substance (by mixing it up) with your own; for this is indeed a great sin. If ye fear that ye shall not be able to deal justly with the orphans, marry (other) women of your choice, two, there, or four. But if ye fear that ye shall not be able to deal justly (with them) then only one, or that which your right hand possess, that will be more suitable to prevent you from doing injustice. (An-Nisaa, 4::2-3)

Muslim caregivers do not need to engage in religious or cultural debates concerning polygamy. Their concern should be how, when, and whether the issue is relevant to the emotional or spiritual well-being of patient or client. This may be one of those situations that tests the skills, beliefs, and core values of the caregiver. Qur'anic mandates are from Allah (swt) as revealed through his Prophet (pbuh). Therefore, in context, polygamous relationships are functional and permitted. They reflect the notion that polygamy provides significant benefit to the individual as well as the community. This benefit ensures that all members of the community are provided for and protected within a family.

Islam and Gay, Lesbian, Bisexual, Transgender and Questioning (GLBTQ) Believers

Introduction

The purpose of this section is to provide non-Muslim caregivers with an overview of concerns related to GLBTQ individuals within the Muslim community. An understanding of the specific challenges of the GLBTQ Muslim can assist you in providing the best care possible. In an encounter, issues the person may disclose possibly include but may not be limited to:

- Rejection by family or community
- Reprisals for their sexual preference(s) or gender reassignment
- Shame and guilt
- Fear and anxiety
- Spiritual distress
- Ego defenses
- Cognitive dissonance

Additionally, young Muslims may actively participate on social media sites. Their participation may present numerous opportunities to network world-wide with other GLBTQ persons (Kelly, 2010). The young Muslims may be inspired to be more vocal and confrontational towards traditional Muslim leaders or values. However, in contrast, the global Muslim community is for the most part consistently resistant to what it perceives as pressure to conform to liberal Western concepts of sexuality, human rights, and fundamental freedoms (Williams, 2010, p.11), (Habib, 2010, pp. xxii-xxiii). Furthermore, Muslims may be concerned about being identified as a part of an overtly white Western middle class social and political movement such as *gay liberation/rights*.

Islamic Considerations

As discussed earlier, Al-Qur'an describes the family as the foundation of the Muslim society. The nuclear family consists of a man, his wife and offspring. There are basic roles necessary to perpetuate a viable Muslim society. In part, the male's function is provide for and protect his family. The female's role is to support her husband and the children. Qur'anicaly, both have separate and collective individual rights and responsibilities. Allah (swt) gave each specific physiological and psychological advantages. Individual communities may vary roles given their own culture, political exigencies, and traditions.

The family, clan, and tribes form the basis of the Islamic Community (Ummah). Behaviors which enhance the community are encouraged. Behaviors that threaten the viability of the community are forbidden. They are forbidden by Al-Qur'an; practices and sayings of the Prophet Muhammad (pbuh) [ahadith]; shari'ah (moral and religious opinions); and local cultural traditions.

Legal sexual intercourse takes place within a *marriage contract* between a man and woman. Illegal intercourse may include adultery, rape, fornication, and homosexuality (primarily anal-penetration). In addition, certain Muslim cultures may have a specifically dress code for men and women that should not be violated. A hadith attributed to the Prophet Muhammad (pbuh) addressed this subject:

> ... (2) The Prophet (Allah bless him and give him peace) cursed effeminate men and masculine women. (3) The Prophet (Allah bless him and give him peace) cursed men who wear women's clothing and women who wear men's. (Al-Misri, 2011, P28.1)

The Qur'anic prohibition against male homosexuality recounts the experience of the Prophet Lut (Lot). This story is similar to the one found in the Hebrew Scriptures. Discussion among Muslim scholars vary as to the exact meaning of the Qur'anic verses. Most commentaries make note of the mistreatment of Lut's quests. Hospitality for travelers was a social obligation in ancient times. Hospitality is still important in Muslims cultures (Al-Baqarah, 2:177). In addition to the hospitality concern, Al-Qur'an suggests that the townsmen desired anal-sex with the guests. This act is still considered an abomination:

> Of all the creatures in the world, will ye approach males and leave those whom Allah has created for you to be your mates? Nay ye are a people transgressing (all limits)! (Ash-Shu'araa, 26:165)

In today's secular culture, the term sodomy is more inclusive than just anal-sex. It may also include oral intercourse between human beings, or any sexual relations between a human being and an animal. However, Islamic traditions define sodomy as anal-penetration. There are prescribed consequences for sodomy. They may range from indeterminate punishments to killings. Lesbian interactions, while prohibited, are not considered as egregious. The Prophet Muhammad (pbuh) revealed the following penalty:

> If two persons among you are guilty of lewdness, punish them both. If they repent and amend, leave them alone for Allah is Oft-returning, Most Merciful. (An-Nisaa, 4:16)

and

> The Prophet (Allah bless him and give him peace) said: (1) "Kill the one who sodomized and the one who lets it be done to him." (2) "May Allah curse him who does what Lot's people did" (3) "Lesbianism by women is adultery between them." (Al-Misr, 2011, P17.3)

It appears that the issue is public awareness of such acts is problematic. The question is, to what extent should a fault/sin be revealed? The Prophet (pbuh) reportedly said that one should cover your brother's faults:

> ...Whoever shields a Muslim, Allah will shield him in this world and the next... (An-Nawawi, Hadith 36)

There is no sacrament of confession in Al-Islam. In certain instances, there may be psychological value in a confession. Confession may bring a certain amount of emotional relief to the individual. It can help to relieve a sense of shame and guilt. Nevertheless, it can be bad for the reputation. It just might get you killed. It is an Islamic principle not to voluntarily divulge or confess a sin. It may be that Allah (swt) has already forgiven the person. Confession would then be a sign of ingratitude to Allah (swt):

> People! The time has come for you to observe the limits of Allah. Whoever has had any of these ugly things befall him should cover them up with the veil of Allah. Whoever reveals his wrong action to us, we will perform what is in the Book of Allah against Him. (Al-Misr, 2011, 41.2.12)

There are some problematic issues surrounding interpretation of Al-Qur'an and the ahadith (exegesis/tafsir). Islamic principles are consistent with revelations given to humans since the time of Prophet Adam (as). Nevertheless, some scholarly interpretations have left many people unsure or confused. This is especially true in relation to gender issues. Progressive Muslims are particularly concerned and seek a modern and broader interpretation of Muslims traditions. Their issues include but are not limited to a pursuit of justice, gender and sexuality, and pluralism (Fadl, 2008). In their quest for a modern understanding, progressive Muslims consider the following:

- Translation of Al-Qur'an from classical Arabic to modern languages
- Cultural bias or narcissism posing as authentic Islamic teaching
- Independent intellectual inquiry into interpretation of religion and Islamic law (ijtihad), and
- Spiritual, mental, and emotional state of an individual (Fadl, 2008, p.33)

Secular GLBTQ Considerations

The scriptures of the Abrahamic religions, Judaism, Christianity, and Al-Islam all oppose sodomy and by extension homosexuality. In America, primarily a Christian county, the Supreme Court (539 U.S.-2003) less than 14 years ago ruled that Texas' *homosexual conduct law*, Penal §21.06, violated the Due Process Clause of the Fourteenth Amendment to the Constitution.

By extension, the Supreme Court nationally decriminalized private consensual intercourse between persons of the same gender. The American Psychiatric Association (APA) removed homosexuality from its Diagnostic and Statistical Manual of Mental Disorders (DSM) in 1973. Also, the APA submitted *amicus curiae* briefs for a number of related Supreme Court cases.

Politically, a number of homosexual advocacy groups have been vocal and active on several issues. Some Muslims have joined these organizations, are sympathizers, or formed their own support groups (Kugle, 2013, p.31). Some less vocal Muslims have taken to visiting chat rooms and other social media (Kramer, 2013, p.134). Some Muslims are ambivalent about participating in public displays such as gay pride parades, or gay marriages. Clinicians may need to take into consideration the extent to which media accounts of attacks, or homosexual persecutions here and abroad, may affect the mental and emotional state of their clients. In terms of immigration challenges, clients may present with fears of returning to the country of their birth, fear of beheadings, entrapment, beatings, arrests, or prison time (Williams, 2010, p.7-9).

Caregiving and Psychological Considerations

I included the foregoing discussion on Al-Qur'an, ahadith, and secular concerns in order to set the stage for recommending an approach to caregiving for GLBTQ Muslims. It is my opinion that clinicians, Muslims and non-Muslims, should be armed with some basic understanding of religious and social determinants which may be a factor in a Muslim clinical encounter. In addition to the clinician's awareness of his/her possible issues of bias and countertransference, he/she should be able to draw upon sound psychological principles. Clinicians have their own arsenal of experiences and training techniques. I offer some perspectives that may be useful.

In my recommendations, I have not taken into account religious prohibition against homosexuality or the nature of sin. They are issues best resolved between the patient and his/her Lord.

I have not directly considered the homosexual political climate, or gay rights groups' advocacy issues. Such groups do not appear to need my advice. My focus is on the possible spiritual, emotional, and psychological clinical distress Muslim homosexuals may present in a clinical encounter. If unaddressed, these conditions may lead to disorders of neurosis, clinical depression, if not suicide. That is unacceptable by any caregiving professional standard. My inspiration for these considerations is found in the *competition in the doing of good* as explained in Al-Baqarah:

> To each is a goal to which Allah turns him; then strive all together (as in a race) towards all that is good. Wheresoever ye are, Allah will bring you together for Allah hath power over all things. (2:148)

Al-Qur'an revealed that we will be judged according to our good deeds, not our sex lives, not what others think of us, nor the degree to which one adheres to prohibitions. It is the righteous (G-d fearing) who will be brought back to Allah (swt) in complete satisfaction:

> ...Nay, nay! But ye honor not the orphans; nor do ye encourage one another to feed the poor; and ye devour inheritance-all with greed, and ye love wealth with inordinate love... (To the righteous will be said) "Oh (thou) soul, in (complete) rest and satisfaction! Come back thou to thy Lord, - well pleased (thyself) and well-pleasing unto Him. Enter thou, then among my Devotees! Yea, enter thou my Heaven!" (Al-Fajr, 17-20, 27-30)

Pleasure and meaning ensue from *doing good*. Dr. Viktor Frankl suggested that the joy from *doing good* cannot be pursued. He suggested that it happens as an existential event in its due time:

> Primarily and normally man does not seek pleasure; instead pleasure –or, for that matter, happiness –is the side effect of living out the self-transcendence of existence. Once one has served a cause or is involved in loving another human being,

happiness occurs by itself. The will to pleasure, however, contradicts the self-transcendent quality of human reality. And it also defeats itself. For pleasure and happiness are by-products. Happiness must be ensued. It cannot be pursued. (Frankl, 2000, 89-90).

Dr. Frankl's observation may be offered to homosexual or transgendered persons as a perspective for coping with societal pressures. Happiness comes from serving a higher cause or loving a person. Sex for the sake of sex whether straight of gay may not bring happiness or satisfaction to an individual. Dr. Frankl continued by describing the intellectual and emotional challenges one can face. These challenges also can apply to homosexuals and transgendered persons:

> Unlike an animal, man is not told by drives and instincts what he must do. And in contrast to man in former times, he is no longer told by traditions and values what he should do. Not, knowing neither what he must do nor what he should do, he sometimes does not basically what he wished to do. Instead he wishes to do what other people wish him to do which is totalitarianism. (Frankl, 2000, p.94)

Islam shapes and defines traditions. These traditions may not be informative for Muslims homosexuals. They may feel that their sex drive is telling them what to do. Instead, the tradition, as currently interpreted by Muslims scholars, does not tell them what they should do concerning their feelings. The person may feel depressed and conflicted. The caregiver or counselor can help the person navigate through his/her sea of confusion to a safe harbor of wellness. There, issues of shame, guilt, and anxiety may then be addressed. Ultimately, the Muslim has to make courageous and conscientious choices to find meaning:

> Traditions and values are crumbling. But meanings are not-cannot be-transmitted by traditions because in contrast to values, which are universal, meanings are unique. As such they are transmitted, mediated to one's consciousness, by

personal conscience. (Frankl, 2000, 118-119)

In my opinion, the psychologist who best describes the challenges of the Muslims homosexual is Abraham Maslow. In his discussion on self-actualization, he touched on many of the challenges they face. In some ways, he agreed with Al-Qur'an. In effect, he addressed the root (fitra) of the personality of the individual, and described it as *unchangeable or unchanging*.

> We have, each of us, an essential biologically based inner nature, which is to some degree "natural," intrinsic, given, and, in a certain limited sense, unchangeable, or, at least, unchanging. (Maslow, 1956, p.3)

There is a question as to whether homosexuality is normal or not. Aside from religion prohibitions, it appears that at least some homosexuals are expressing their inner nature or predisposition (fitra). This predisposition in itself is not basically evil. Perhaps, it is an expression of a need to become a fully actualized individual. If not addressed or fully expressed, it may lead to mental health issues or destructive behaviors.

> This inner nature, as much as we know of it so far, seems not to be intrinsically or primarily or necessarily evil. The basic needs (for life, for safety and security, for belongingness and affection, for respect and self-respect, and for self-actualization), the basic human emotions and the basic human capacities are on their face either neutral, pre-moral or positively "good." Destructiveness, sadism, cruelty, malice, etc., seem so far to be not intrinsic but rather they seem to be violent reactions against frustration of our intrinsic needs, emotions and capacities. (Maslow, 1956, p.3)

The religious prohibitions against Muslim homosexuality do not address the psychological need of the individual or recommend coping skills. The inner nature (fitra) of the individual is good or neutral. Individuals require copings skills to navigate feelings of rejection, being ostracized, or harassment, in order to obtain spiritual wellbeing:

> Since this inner nature is good or neutral rather than bad, it is best to bring it out and to encourage it rather than to suppress it. If it is permitted to guide our life, we grow healthy, fruitful, and happy. (Maslow, 1956, p.3)

Dr. Maslow succinctly summarized the challenges that Muslim homosexuals have to face in the Muslim community, and the American society in general. A healthy society produces healthy people:

> Sick people are made by a sick culture; healthy people are made possible by a heathy culture. But it is just as true that sick individuals make their culture more sick (sic) and that healthy individuals make their culture more healthy. (Maslow, 1956, p.5)

Summary

In summary, Muslim GLBTQ believers are still a part of the community (ummah). As such, their challenges, emotional and spiritual health should be addressed in the best manner possible by the Muslim community:

> Invite (all) to the Way of thy Lord with wisdom and beautiful preaching. And, argue with them in ways that are best and most gracious. For thy Lord knoweth best who have strayed from His Path, and who receive guidance. (An-Nahl, 16:125)

Caregivers and clinicians appear to be on the forefront of providing compassionate care to Muslim homosexuals. Perhaps this discussion can assists them in understanding the challenges Muslims homosexuals face within the Muslim community as well as the society in general. The Muslim community appears to be in a quandary in regards to responding to Muslims homosexuals in an *open secular society*. The community may not be able to make a distinction between the Qur'anic *letter of the law* and the spiritual care and well-being requirements of the individual. Inshallah, Allah (swt) in His mercy will provide guidance to the community as necessary. Nevertheless, caregivers and clinicians have an opportunity and professional responsibility to address and provide care for Muslim GLBTQ individuals. May Allah (swt) guide us all to the betterment of His people.

Al-Khalifah and Developing Communities of Peace and Justice

In America, today, and in the West in particular, the concept of Al-Khalifah, the Muslim society, is not well understood. Caregivers who interact with Muslim patients and clients may benefit from an understanding and appreciation of a khalifah from an Islamic perspective. The following information may assist you in developing a spiritual construct for assisting the patient. Please note that historic and current events, your attitudes, and politics may affect your encounter.

As I prepare this work, the US media is replete with print and television coverage of the Islamic State of Iraq and Syria (ISIS). ISIS has declared itself a worldwide Khalifah. In Nigeria, Boko Haram has done the same. The vast majority of Muslims worldwide reject these notions. Certainly, there is the possibility that caregivers to Muslims unduly may be influenced by the media. This fact can lead to countertransference which should be avoided. In the larger sense, media bias, mischief making, and unbalanced reporting can lead to or encourage public xenophobia, Islamophobia, and ignorance.

What is the Qur'anic definition of a Khalifah? In the Yusuf Ali translation, the word khalifah is defined as *vicegerent* (Note 988, MHE, p.395). This word, in more contemporary language, can be interpreted as deputy or successor. In this sense, a deputy is a person who has the authority to represent and enforce legal statutes, social justice, customary laws, and to protect property rights. From an Islamic perspective, human beings are the deputies (vicegerents) of Allah (swt) on earth. In addition, they are Allah's (swt) trustees for the environment, nature, animals, and other resources.

The purpose of a khalifah is to establish communities of peace and justice according to Allah's (swt) guidance as revealed in Al-Qur'an. By doing so, society may prosper:

> Allah has promised, to those among you who believe and work righteous deeds, that He will, of a surety, grant them in the land inheritance (of power), as He granted it to those before them; that He will establish in authority their religion -the one which He has chosen for them; and, that He will change their state, after the fear in which they lived, to one of security and peace. They will worship Me (alone) and not associate aught with Me. If any do reject faith after this, they are rebellious and wicked. (An-Nur, 24:55)

Traditionally, the authority of the khalifah rested in the Prophet Muhammad (pbuh). He can be considered the first Khalif (Caliph). In addition to receiving revelation from Allah (swt), he functioned as Leader/Defender of the Faithful. The Prophets Musa (as) and Dawud (as), peace be upon them both, shared similar mandates. Furthermore, some Muslim scholars still debate the Qur'anic meaning of khalifah. There is a discussion among them whether it is a political entity, or solely the moral leadership of the Ummah (Khan, 1982). After the death of the Prophet Muhammad (pbuh), the leadership of Khalifs continued up to the destruction and dismantling of the Ottoman (Turkish) Empire at the end of World War 1.

During World War1, the Ottoman Empire allied with the Central Powers of the Kaiser (Germany) and the Austria-Hungarian Empire against United Kingdom, France, Russia, and the US. During the war, promises of national independence possibly influenced ethnic rebellions against the Ottomans. Upon their defeat, the Allies dismantled the Ottoman Empire thereby creating the modern Arab States and the Republic of Turkey.

The League of Nations (LON) granted France mandates over Syria and Lebanon. The United Kingdom received mandates over Mesopotamia (later called Iraq,) and Palestine. Subsequently, LON divided Palestine. It then became Palestine and Transjordan. The former Ottoman Empire territories on the Arabian Peninsula became the Kingdom of Hejaz and the Sultanate of Nejd (today Saudi Arabia); the Kingdom of Yemen, and the Arab States of the Persian Gulf.

The British occupied Palestine in 1919. In 1923, they officially administered a Palestine Mandate from the LON. The Mandate reaffirmed the 1917 British commitment to the Balfour Declaration. The Balfour Declaration supported the establishment in Palestine of a national home for the Jewish people. The United Nations (formerly LON) denied Palestinian independence (as promised by the Allies). Instead, after the British withdrew, Western powers allowed Jewish Zionist to declare and establish the State of Israel in 1948. As a result, today there is still unrest in the Middle East as well as efforts underway by some ethnic groups to reassemble a khalifah in the Middle East. (Hossein, 1997, p.12-15, 25-28).

Many Muslims carry a *collective spiritual memory* of a society which closely followed the dictates of Al-Qur'an. In some ways, the historical memory of the crusades waged by the West, and the dissolution of the Ottoman Khalifah lurk in the *shadow memory* of both Muslims and Christians (Huntington, 1997). Caregivers may find the forgoing information useful for assessing their own possible issues of countertransference. Additional, the client may communicate or transfer feelings of mistrust and anger to the caregiver.

According to Al-Qur'an, the goals of the khalifah are to establish Communities of Peace and Justice; secure a safe place for the completion of doing of good; provide for and protect families; and serve as an example for mankind. These actions will go a long way to remove much of the emotional stress/anxiety, mischief, grief, and destructive behaviors that impair both Muslims and non-Muslims societies. Whether one considers the khalifah as a political entity, or as a leadership community, there is much inspiration, healing and comfort for the humanity in the following verse:

It is He Who hath made you the inheritors of the earth; He hath raised you in ranks, some above others, that he may try you in the gifts He hath given you; for thy Lord is quick in punishment; yet He is indeed Oft-forgiving, Most Merciful. (Al-An'am, 6:165)

In summary, the khalifah should represent the legal authority that implements the guidelines revealed in Al-Qur'an through the Prophet Muhammad (pbuh). Historical events such as crusades, colonization, internal rivalries, tribal hegemony, mischief makers, and hypocrisies have gone a long way to undermine the original guidance for a khalifah. Caregivers should be mindful that they may be challenged by distortions of the meaning of khalifah by the Western media, Islamophobias, and misguided Muslims.

Chapter 5: Identifying the Spiritual Roots of Terrorism

Whosoever of you sees an evil action, let him change it with his hand; and if he is not able to do so, then with his tongue; and if he is not able to do so, then with his heart — and that is the weakest of faith.

-Prophet Muhammad, An-Nawawi, Hadith, No.34

Some of these chronically misunderstood people retreat into religion, where they proceed to do exactly as they did before. They complain and commiserate with themselves, shifting the burdens onto the shoulders of a benevolent God. They think only about themselves. It is therefore natural for them to believe that God, this extraordinary honored and worshipped being, is concerned entirely with servicing them and is responsible for their every action...They approach their god just as they approach their fellow human beings, complaining, whining, yet never lifting a finger to help themselves or to better their circumstances. Cooperation, they feel, is an obligation only for others.

-Abraham H. Maslow, Toward a Psychology of Being, p. 214

Introduction

I have noticed that one of the greatest challenges of the 21st century is for clinicians of every discipline to arrive at an acceptable definition of the word *terrorism*, and by extension, the word *terrorist*. In my opinion, dictionary definitions are no longer adequate. They do they take into consideration American cultural and ideological/political concerns, or the psycho-social-spiritual perspective of those most affected by acts of terrorism. Terrorism usually means or suggests some threat of violence and/or psychological persecution against an innocent person. In a military sense, it usually refers to actions against the non-combatant civilian population. Feelings on this subject run high and threaten the social fabric of the American Society.

I am passionate about this issue, primarily because of personal experience. I witnessed the attack on the World Trade Center (WTC) on September 11, 2001. With a bird's-eye-view from the 23rd floor of a federal office building several blocks from the site, I saw the destruction caused by the first plane. The second plane actually flew by several hundred feet from the federal building on its way to the second tower. Once I realized the seriousness of the event, I felt that the federal building was a possible alternate target. With thousands of others, I experienced the panic of that life-threatening situation. I managed with others to escape the area shortly before the two buildings fell. As a Muslim leader in the Interfaith Community, I felt the pressure to explain to my colleagues, the inexplicable behavior of misguided Muslim attackers. And, as an imam and Muslim pastoral counselor, I had to minister to and address the religious and spiritual needs of my own Community.

I cannot speak for the actions of others, nor fully address such a comprehensive and complex subject such as terrorism. Only Allah (swt) in His infinite wisdom has the complete understanding. Nevertheless, as a Muslim pastoral counselor and chaplain, I offer to you several Qur'anic and clinical observations. The general discussion of terrorism and so-called *Islamic terrorism* in particular, currently floods the airways, as well as the minds of many Americans. This discussion can be quite unsettling for American Muslims. The reasons are many. I suggest a few:

- Muslims seem to be colored by the labels of Islamic terrorists, Muslim Fundamentalists, etc., in the same manner that Black or Latino persons can be tainted by the criminal actions of a few misguided members of their respective communities
- Gross ignorance on the part of the general American public concerning the extent to which Muslims appreciate the sanctity of life, the religion of Al-Islam, and the building of communities founded on peace and justice
- Continuous mistrust, cross-talk, and inauthentic communication
- Destructive actions of mischief-makers (Muslims and non-Muslims) who foment discord for political reasons and/or evil intentions, as well as purposes of self-aggrandizement
- Seemingly, the federal government's disregard and/or denial of the adverse effects of *collateral damage* to civilians/non-combatants during *seek and destroy* missions/drone missile strikes
- Unresolved feelings of grief, pain, anger, and helplessness of some individual Muslims/Communities related to issues of loss of non-combatant life. i.e. family, friends, as well as property
- Rendition practices, and certain seemingly *arbitrary and capricious* government surveillance tactics
- Community impression or feeling of being under siege by several enforcement agencies.

Any attempt to fully address the aforementioned concerns amounts to a formidable task beyond the purview of this work. The following discussion focuses on pastoral and clinical care concepts, and strategies for Muslim patients and clients given the current American political climate. Nevertheless, it may be impossible to avoid mention of certain aspects of the aforementioned issues. They may be intricately intertwined into, or present themselves in a psycho-social-spiritual assessment.

Oppression Is Worse Than Death

Oppression in any form is expressly forbidden in the religion of Al-Islam. There is no excuse or justification for it. There is an authentic hadith of the Prophet Muhammad (pbuh) recorded in *Sahih Muslim*. It is reported that the Prophet Muhammad (pbuh) narrated that Allah (swt) stated that He has expressly forbidden oppression, even for Himself. Accordingly, He forbids mankind to oppress one another:

> Oh My servants, I have forbidden oppression (dhulm) for Myself, and I have made it forbidden amongst you, so do not oppress one another. Oh My servants, all of you are astray except those whom I have guided, so seek guidance from Me and I shall guide you... (An-Nawawi. Hadith 24)

It is well known that there are some people, who for reasons or feelings of their own, appear to offer up their lives in the face of oppression or persecution. For example, individual soldiers have been known to throw themselves onto unexploded devices in order to protect their fellow troops. Persons labeled as heroes have been known to put themselves *in harm's way* in order to come to the aid of helpless victims being harassed or robbed. And, a father or mother may act to protect their family by stepping in front of their child when the family is caught in urban gunfire. These are examples and situations of individuals who are willing to sacrifice their lives for an apparent *higher cause*.

Over the years, the press and government officials have reported on horrendous acts of violence. Often, many lives were lost. During investigations, it has been discovered that some of these atrocities have been perpetrated by individuals who self–identify as Muslim. Western media, politicians, and the general public are challenged to find language to give meaning to these acts. Eventually, they settle on some language for the public discourse.

Each interest group has its *term of art*. Given recent

American military history in the Middle East, politicians and the military often use the terms *Islamic Fundamentalist*, *Muslim Terrorist*, *Islamist*, *Muslim Fundamentalist*, and others. Each term can have its own political currency or useful effect on voters. To my knowledge, no politician, military, or government official has thought to ask the Muslim Community to define the character of these people. For the most part, the Community has been asked to apologize for, or to explain the behavior of the individual perpetrator.

Certainly, there have been a number of terrible act over the last few years committed by religious or non-religious people. Some of them identified themselves as Muslim. There is enough blame to around. And, responsible media may seek to find some middle ground in order to project a balanced and unbiased definition/reporting.

Many Muslims object to being vicariously labeled terrorists. Muslims are a minority group in the US. They are not in control of major media outlets. They do not have enough political clout to effectively advance their own terms of art in the market place of idea. As a result, they may be splattered with paint from the same brush used to color some Muslim mischief-makers.

There exists a plethora of general information in the media, as well as scholarly publications concerning terrorists/terrorism. However, there appears to be a paucity of relevant psycho-social-spiritual analyses on the subject. This fact may be important for Muslim caregivers and clinicians. They may encounter patients and clients who are vicariously traumatized, or at least anxious at the possibility of being painted with the *terrorist brush*. There are very few places for the clinician to look for culturally significant information to help assess, investigate, or maintain the spiritual/mental health of American Muslims.

The exact reason(s) that a person offers up his or her life for a cause in a so-called terrorist act remains with Allah (swt) alone. It may have something to do with the mental and emotional state of a person. From an Islamic perspective, *fighting in the cause of Allah (swt) is definitely permitted*. Accordingly, how, and to what extent, does a person separate Allah's (swt) cause, from the person's self-righteous ego?

In Al-Qur'an, Allah (swt) set limits on fighting engagements as well as the manner in which one should fight. Al-Qur'an clearly states that *persecution is worse than slaughter*.

> Fight in the cause of Allah those who fight you but do not transgress limits; for Allah loveth not transgressors. And slay them wherever ye catch them and turn them out from where they have turned you out; for persecution is worse than slaughter…(Al-Baqarah, 2:190-191)

The verse implies that persecution itself is already a form of torture. It suggests that death is an option for assuaging the possible debilitating depression or neurosis attendant to persistent persecution. In a secular vein, the playwright William Shakespeare offers a similar meaning in his play *Julius Caesar*:

> A coward dies a thousand times before his death, the valiant never taste of death but once. Of all the wonders that I yet have heard, it seems to me most strange that men should fear, seeing that death, a necessary end, will come when it will come. (Shakespeare, 1919, p. 36)

Dr. Abraham Maslow, author of the concept of the *hierarchy of needs* further discussed the possible mental health condition of such individuals. Consistent with the teachings of Al-Qur'an, he suggested that submission to oppression can in itself be a sign of a mental disorder:

> In essence I am deliberately rejecting our present easy distinction between sickness and health, at least as far as surface symptoms are concerned…In a word if you tell me you have a personality problem I am not certain until I know you better whether to say "good" or "I'm sorry." It depends on the reason. And, these it seems, may be bad reasons, or they may be good reasons…. Clearly what will be called personality problems depends on who is doing the

> calling...What is sick then is not to protest while this crime is being committed. (Maslow, 2011, p. 6-7)

A clear understanding of scripture related to oppression may be helpful in addressing the spiritual needs of the patient or client. Along these lines, there are a few significant verses that may be useful. In search for justice, the Muslims may look for compensation from competent authorities for the acts of oppression; for example, in the unjustified death of a loved-one, e.g. collateral damage. The *turn-the-other-cheek* philosophy, popular among some Christians, is not necessarily a Muslim spiritual perspective. The Muslim psyche may require, if not demand, reasonable compensation or emotional satisfaction.

> Oh ye who believe, the law of equity is prescribed for you in cases of murder. The free for the free, the slave for the slave, the woman for the woman; but if any remission is made by the brother of the slain, then grant any reasonable demand, and compensate him with handsome gratitude. This is a concession and a Mercy from your Lord. After this whoever exceeds the limits shall be in grave chastisement. (Al-Baqarah, 2:178)

The family, and by extension the tribe, is extremely important to many Muslims. Protection of the family is paramount. An inability to provide for and protect the family may be internalized as a serious problem for the men of the family. This need to protect may manifest at times when a family member is in need of healthcare services. It may appear that the husband/father is insinuating himself into the provision of services for a family member. He may feel that as the provider or protector of the family, it is his obligation. A knowledgeable and savvy healthcare worker should be able to discuss the issues with him in a professional manner. The relevant verse from Al-Qur'an follows:

> Men are the protectors and maintainers of women...(An-Nisaa, 4:34)

Qur'anic Right of Self-Defense

According to Al-Qur'an, the right to self-defense is inalienable. It is basic, and is intended to assure the continued viability of the Community. Accordingly, Allah (swt) set limits on reprisals. There is a commandment for equity and justice. Its objective is to make the aggrieved individual whole once again, and not to take undue advantage of the situation:

> ...There is a law of equity. If then any one transgresses the prohibition against you, transgress ye likewise against him. But, fear Allah, and know that Allah is with those who restrain themselves. (Al-Baqarah, 2:194)

Fighting is permissible for those who have been persecuted or attacked solely because of their religion:

> To those against whom war is made, permission is given (to fight), because they are wronged; and verily Allah is Most Powerful for their aid; (They are) those who have been expelled from their homes in defiance of right, for no cause except that they say, "Our Lord is Allah..." (Al-Hajj, 22:39-40)

Al-Qur'an is clear that fighting should be for self-defense, and that the Muslims should not be the aggressor under any circumstance. The blame for the offense rests with the aggressor(s). In any event, forgiveness, when it is possible, is encouraged:

> The recompense for an injury is an injury equal thereto (in degree): but if a person forgives and makes reconciliation, his reward is due from Allah; for (Allah) loveth not those who do wrong. But indeed, if any do help and defend himself after a wrong (done) to him, against such there is no cause of blame. (Ash-Shura, 42:40-41)

Individual Psychology Verses Sociology and Terrorism

Only Allah (swt) knows what is the mind and heart of a person. Ultimately, He will judge each one of us according to his/her actions. He will bestow His Grace and Mercy on those whom He sees fit according to His own Will. He is the Best Knower of all the facts and *truth* of the matter. Allah (swt) has given us tools to assess behavior. This is a part of His Ar-Rahman (Beneficence).

It is natural for human beings to want to be in control of their lives. The factors use to determine that which leads a person to commit acts of violence should be identified on an individual case-by-case basis. To my knowledge, there is not an extensive data base or clinical cases that thoroughly address the acts of terrorism. Indeed, depending on the cultural bias and/or political environment, one man's terrorist might be considered another man's hero.

In the United States, clinical mental health analysis primarily is based upon criteria in the Diagnostic and Statistical Manual of Mental Health Disorders (DSM-5 TM). The American Psychiatric Association (APA) published its most recent version in 2013. The DSM-5 TM offers criteria for various psychological disorders including but not limited to schizophrenia, anxiety disorders, personality disorders, and others. There is a question as to whether terrorists generally have a mental disorder. Perhaps, the day will come when the there is enough valid data to produce an informed opinion and criteria for identifying and defining a *terroristic personality disorder*. It will be interesting to see whether the final definition of such a disorder will be purely clinical, or whether it will be based on Western cultural bias.

The DSM-5 TM gives us a clue of changes to come in future revisions. It includes discussions on mental disorders and their relationship to cultural, social, and familial norms and values. It includes narratives on Cultural Formation. It identifies and explains: Cultural syndrome; Cultural idiom of distress; and Cultural explanation or perceived cause. (APA, 2013, p.14). It is my prayer that given the importance of the discussion of so-called Islamic terrorism, Muslim extremists, and other such terms, Muslim clinicians will have input in future revisions. To this effect, I recommend the following:

- The APA immediately begin to involve Muslims in cultural and clinical dialogue in preparation for future revisions (DSM-5 TM-R), and
- That Muslim clinicians/clinical pastoral educators organize and be prepared to engage the APA on the role and limitation of religion and culture in mental health diagnosis.

I do not believe that people are born with the desire to become terrorists. There is a Hadith of the Prophet Muhammad (pbuh) that in parts suggests that every child is born with goodness and G-d consciousness (Bewley. 2011, p.92). It is his/her parents who shape the child's understanding of religion. By extension, this also may be true of society and its influence on terroristic behavior.

Dr. Sigmund Freud suggested that even though a person is seeking to satisfy his instinctual impulses he cannot overlook the influences of other people. This suggests that society as a whole bears some responsibility for one another's behavior:

> ...only rarely and under certain exceptional conditions is individual psychology in a position to disregard the relations of this individual to others. In the individual's mental life someone else is invariably involved, as a model, as an object, as a helper, as an opponent.

He further stated that the condition:

> ...is at the same time social psychology as well. (Freud, 1959, p.3)

In understanding issues of terroristic behavior, there are at least two major psychological concerns. Notwithstanding notions of politics and cultural/societal prejudices, and assuming there is no obvious present history of mental illness these are: 1) the mindset and understanding of the individual psychology of the alleged terrorist, and 2) the social-spiritual dynamic present. Intelligent and reliable analysis of these concerns may not be possible at this time given the paucity of psychological data on terrorists.

Terrorists and Narcissistic Traits

From a psychological perspective, terrorists may often act out their *narcissistic* tendencies. This is possible to the extent that they disregard the inalienable rights of life, liberty and the pursuit of happiness of the people they affect. Even if the terrorist believes he/she is justified, the person nevertheless acts from a narcissistic perspective. That is, their individual instinct takes precedence. Accordingly, this entitles him/her to impose his/her will (Lerner, 2009, p. xi).

As stated earlier, Al-Qur'an explicitly requires justice in deliberating grievances, forgiveness where possible, and puts limits on violence necessary to achieve justice. The objective is to make the person whole once more, and to achieve spiritual and emotional wellbeing. Muslims who commit terroristic acts are subjected to these Qur'anic criteria and accordingly will be held accountable by Allah (swt) on the Day of Judgement. In the meantime, righteous and law abiding Muslims have the responsibility to oppose Muslim and non-Muslim terrorists who violate Allah's (swt) mandates.

Terrorism and Group Psychology

There appears to be at least two major paths taken by terrorists. One is the path of the *lone wolf*. This path is most often identified with a *suicide bomber*. On the other path, a terrorist may act in concert with his compatriots/co-conspirators. It may be said that the second path is traveled by what I term *socio-narcissists*. For the purpose of this work, socio-narcissists are a group of people of like-mind who individually meet the criteria for a Narcissistic Personality Disorder (NPD), or narcissistic traits. They act in concert under the influence and suggestibility of a group. Dr. Wilfred Trotter in part addressed aspects of social-narcissism in his book *Instincts of the Herd in Peace and War*. (Trotter, 1921) Dr. Sigmund Freud referred often to Trotter's concept of *the herding instinct* as it related to the *group mind*. Also, Dr. Freud quoted the noted sociologist Gustave Le Bon on various aspects of the characteristics of *crowds*. (Le Bon, 2002). In summary, these authors discussed psychological and sociological aspects of the group mind. By extension, they included the group mind of terrorists. Potential terrorist can be susceptible to the group mind. This points to how the group can influence individual behavior in ways that an individual would not behave on his/her own. Finally, terrorists can be greatly influenced by the suggestibility of a group leader (Le Bon, 2002, p. 6-7).

Reflection

In summary, it is easy to understand how the American Muslim Community as a whole can be challenged religiously, spiritually, and emotionally by accusations of terrorism. There is pressure from the Christian and Jewish Communities on *moderate* Muslims to somehow magically divine which individual Muslim in the community will respond violently to Islamophobia, suspicion, name-calling, anger and unresolved grief. Again, moderate Muslims are expected to lead the charge against terrorism. The American society expects them to do so without an adequate public discourse addressing all identifiable political component parts of terroristic behaviors. It appears that any hesitation on the part of an individual Muslim, or Muslim Communities to get swept up in the emotional political fray of anti-terrorist rhetoric without necessary reflection, assessment and analysis of the issues is considered un-American. As caregivers, clinicians and educators, we should concern ourselves with meeting the psycho-socio-spiritual well-being of patients and clients. Our objective should be to promoting the betterment of the human condition. Our challenge is to bring a sane analysis to the discussion of terrorism and the psycho-socio-spiritual needs of Muslim clients and patients.

Al-Qur'an states that it is in the very nature of men and women to be rebellious. Inevitably, a part of the human experience includes mischief –making and shedding of blood (Al-Baqarah,

2:30). It is precisely because of our imperfect nature that Prophets throughout the ages have delivered guidance from the Deity. Ultimately, the Creator will be the final judge of our individual and collective actions. Fear is a *gift* from the Creator. It is a part of being human. It lets us know that there is imminent danger. We cannot always control the emotion of fear. However, we can seek to understand and address the fear of terrorism and work to improve the human condition.

> It may be that Allah will establish friendship between you and those whom ye (now) hold as enemies; for Allah has power (over all things); and Allah is Oft-Forgiving Most Merciful. Do men think that they will be left alone on saying, "We believe," and that they will not be tested? We did test those before them, and Allah will certainly know those who are true from those who are false. (Al-Ankabut, 29:2-3)

May we survive the tests of Allah (swt) and continue to build communities of peace and justice in America; and the people of G-d say, "Amen."

Chapter 6: Al-Islam and Clinical Analysis

Whosoever removes a worldly grief from a believer, Allah will remove from him one of the griefs of the Day of Judgement. Whoever alleviates [the lot of] a needy person, Allah will alleviate [his lot] in this world and the next. Whosoever shields a Muslim, Allah will shield him in this world and the next. And Allah will aid a servant [of His] so long as he aids his brother. Whosoever follows a path to seek knowledge therein, Allah will make easy for him a path to Paradise. No people gather together in one of the Houses of Allah, reciting the Book of Allah and studying it among themselves, without tranquility descending upon them, and mercy enveloping them, and the angels surround them, and Allah making mention of them amongst those who are with Him. Whosoever is slowed down by his actions, will not be hastened forward by his lineage.

-Prophet Muhammad, An-Nawawi, Hadith, No. 36

In any psychotherapy, the therapist himself is a highly important part of the human equation. What he does, the attitude he holds, his basic concept of his role, all influence therapy to a marked degree. Different therapeutic orientations hold differing views on these points...The primary point of the importance here is the attitude held by the counselor toward the worth and significance of the individual. How do we look at others? Do we see each person as having worth and dignity in his own right? If we do hold this point of view at the verbal level, to what extent is it operationally evident at the behavioral level? Do we tend to treat individuals as persons of worth, or do we subtly devaluate them by our attitudes and behaviors?

-Rogers, Carl R., Client, Centered Therapy, p. 19- 20

Caregiving from an Islamic Perspective

The purpose of this chapter is to provide useful clinical techniques for addressing the psycho-socio-spiritual needs of Muslims. I based my observations and recommendations on selected Islamic resources, primarily Al-Qur'an and ahadith, as well as my own professional experience. Some clinicians may believe that clinical assessment derives from relatively recent secular scientific notions. However, I do not agree. From primordial times to the present, peoples have asked questions, sought answers, and made assessments about human behaviors and emotions. Dr. Bruce Bynum suggested that ancient texts discussed this evolutionary path to self-discovery:

> The ancient texts agree that a spiritual force animates human existence and evolution itself. Evolution is more than random selection and capricious adaptation. There is a luminous unfoldment from more subtle realms or order. The perennial testimony is that there is a path and a multiplicity of paths on the One Path to self-discovery and illumination. (Bynum, 2012, xxiv)

As Muslims, we believe that the wisdom of the ancients culminates in the revelation of Al-Qur'an. This wisdom can help to remove spiritual roadblocks, detours, and emotional traffic jams in our lives. We view the book as a mercy, guidance, and a spiritual operator's manual.

> Oh mankind, there hath come to you an admonition from your Lord and a healing for the (diseases) in your hearts, and for those who believe, Guidance and a Mercy. Say "In the Bounty of Allah and His Mercy, in that let them rejoice;" that is better than the wealth they hoard. (Yunus, 10:57-58)

Al-Qur'an is not a medical or science book. Nevertheless, it alludes to medical information not discovered until hundreds of years after the revelation. Scientists discovered the significance of the cognitive functions of the frontal lobes. It is known that the processes for making plans, moral decisions, and choices for behavior take place in the frontal lobes (Ibrahim, 1991, p.16). Al-Qur'an mentions that the human mind has the potential to distinguish truth from falsehood. It suggests that this ability takes place in the *forelock*. From a Qur'anic perspective, the frontal lobes (forelock) are the place where lying and deceitful behaviors can formulate.

> Seest thou if he denies (truth) and turns away? Knoweth he not that Allah doth see? Let him beware! If he desist not, We will drag him by the forelock, a lying, sinful forelock. (Iqraa, 96:13-14)

For the Muslim, true happiness and peace of mind, body and soul can only be realized by submitting to the commandments of the Creator and Sustainer of the Worlds, and His guidance. From a caregiving perspective, Al-Qur'an contains all the spiritual direction and strategies for addressing our needs as well as promoting spiritual healing:

> We send down (stage by stage) of the Qur'an that which is a healing and a mercy to those who believe; to the unjust it causes nothing but loss after loss. (Bani Isra'il, 17:82)

Al-Qur'an states that when a person submits himself/herself to Allah's guidance, and performs good deeds according to His direction, emotions of fear, grief, possibly anxiety, and depression will be relieved.

> Nay, whoever submits his whole self to Allah and is the doer of good, he will get his reward with his Lord; on such will be no fear nor shall they grieve. (Al-Baqarah, 2:112)

Caregivers may be able to address the emotional and spiritual needs of Muslim patients by knowing how some Muslims perceive their relationship to Al-Islam. When exploring feeling and emotions it may be useful to listen to *living human document,* and use Socratic questioning. Please be aware that believers differ in their understanding and commitment to Al-Islam, as in any religion.

Nevertheless, Al-Qur'an defines a true believer as the one who feels Allah (swt) in his/her heart:

> For believers are those who when Allah is mentioned feel a tremor in their hearts; and when they hear His revelations rehearsed, find their faith strengthen, and put (all) their trust in their Lord. (Al-Anfal, 8:2)

It may be that in the future, scientist will discover a source of neurotransmitters such as dopamine or serotonin in the heart. This will help to better understand the Qur'anic perspective of heart as the seat of human feelings. There already exists scientific data on neurotransmitters in other parts of the body such as the enteric nervous system (Gershon, 1998, viii).

Al-Qur'an is more than a religious document. Some Muslims use it as an *operator's manual* for day-to-day living. As such, Al-Qur'an is the resource for addressing human behavior. One of the attributes of Allah (swt) is The Guidance (Al-Huda). Accordingly, His revealed book includes mandates and procedures for resolving human emotional and mental conflicts

Today, not much of the Book is left to the individual Muslims to interpret. One usually defers to recognized scholars from various respected religious schools of law. These schools are Hanafi, Maliki, Shafi'i, and Hanbali. Collectively, these are the Sunni schools of jurisprudence. The Ja'fari school of law represents Shia jurisprudence. These schools are identical in at least 75% of their rulings (Al-Misri, n.d., p.vii). At issue is the extent to which their ancient rulings reflect the *true meaning and intent* as revealed in the time of the Prophet Muhammad (pbuh). Subsequently, Progressive Muslims sometimes question the relevance of particular rulings for issues in the 21st century. To further complicate the matter, Al-Qur'an has been translated into hundreds of modern languages. This fact can further complicate scriptural hermeneutics (tafsir). While the exact meaning of a word or a phrase may be disputed, the spirit of the meaning can still be captured and expressed in any language.

To the Muslim, Allah's (swt) Guidance, transmitted and

revealed in Al-Qur'an, holds the keys to good mental and emotional health. This point is confirmed as follows:

> Verily, We have revealed the Book to thee in Truth, for (instructing) mankind. He, then, that receives guidance benefits his own soul. But he that strays injures his own soul. Nor art thou a custodian over them. (Sad, 39:41)

Islamicly, emotions and behaviors related to fear, anxiety, repressed desires, thinking errors, drug usage, social dysfunction, and other challenges to the soul, primarily reside in the *spiritual heart*. When the spiritual heart is not in accord with the dictates of Allah (swt), the human being is in a state of disorder. This disorder may manifest itself in suffering or discomfort.

The clinicians should be aware that for some Muslims, behaviors such missing or abandoning any of the required five daily prayers (salaat), not fasting during Ramadan; illegal drug use and/or alcohol consumption; sex outside of marriage; homosexuality; and deliberately missing Friday congregational prayer (Jummah) may be a cause of spiritual stress or discomfort. Additionally, contemporary cultural challenges related to public ridicule from wearing cultural clothes (e.g. hijab); disparaging media representation of Muslims or Al-Islam; and concomitant issues of shame and guilt; may present during consultations.

The spiritual heart of those who continue to drift from Allah's guidance is prone to a spiritual disease. Al-Qur'an suggests that the greater the distance from the guidance a person is, the greater the potential for disease and further spiritual complications:

> In their hearts is a disease and Allah has increased their disease, and grievous is the chastisement they incur because the lied (to themselves). (Al-Baqarah, 2:10)

Fundamental Spiritual Concerns

Introduction

Similar to Christian and Jewish scriptures, Al-Qur'an can be useful as a therapeutic tool for addressing Muslim patients and clients. It contains images, narratives, metaphors, and directives for holistic care. Many non-Muslim caregivers do not fully appreciate or understand the commitment of Muslims to Allah (swt), the religion of Al-Islam, the Qur'an, and the ahadith. Muslims believe that life, death, fortunes, and misfortunes are predestined. We refer to this matter as the *qadar* of Allah (swt), i.e. divine preordainment:

> No misfortune can happen on earth or in your souls but is recorded in a Book before We bring it into existence, that is truly easy for Allah, in order that ye may not despair over matters that pass you by; nor exult over favors bestowed upon you; for Allah loveth not any vainglorious boaster. (Al-Hadid, 57:22-23)

The qadar of Allah (swt) suggests that Allah (swt) decreed all matters into existence and knows exactly when and where everything will occur. This includes all our joys as well as all our sufferings. This preordainment is manifested in the use of the expression *mashallah* (it is as Allah wills). Therefore, life is a challenge and a test. Our obligation is to persevere in the guidance given to us and to find meaning in joy as well as unavoidable suffering.

> Be sure We shall test you with something of fear and hunger, some loss in goods, lives and the fruits (of your toil), but give glad tidings to those who patiently persevere, who say, when afflicted with calamity, "To Allah we belong, and to Him is our return." They are those on whom (descend) blessings from their Lord, and Mercy; and they are the ones that receive guidance. (Al-Baqarah, 2:155-157)

It is a Muslim's duty to adhere to the fundamentals of Al-Islam. At times, the pressure of popular American culture can challenge one's belief and appear to be at odds with Islamic practices. Some of these challenges include social drinking, recreational marijuana, and liberal interaction between men and women. Certain Muslims may succumb to these pressures. The result may precipitate an identity crisis. The severity of the crisis may vary depending on how strictly the family practices fundamentals of the religion. Young Muslims may be more accommodating to popular culture; especially, if they were born in the US. Also, they may be less bothered by the apparent conflict. Older immigrant Muslims may be less tolerant.

Creation Story: Adam and His Mate

Although there are some similarities, the story of the creation in Al-Qur'an differs significantly from Beresit in the Torah/Genesis in Christian Bible. An appreciation of the differences may help the clinician to understand better the Islamic concept of sin and forgiveness. In the Qur'an, there is no taking of a rib from Prophet Adam (as). There is no blaming of Eve. In fact, Eve is not mentioned by name. The revelation refers to Eve as *thy wife* (in Arabic, *zoujuka*).

Al-Qur'an describes a conversation between Allah (swt) and His angels. The conversations centered on the nature of humankind. Angels in Al-Islam are rational beings who can question. However, they do not have free-will to oppose Allah (swt). They must so as He commands. The angels questioned Allah (swt) about his intention to create humankind, a species which would cause mischief in the world, and have a violent nature.

> Behold! Thy Lord said to the angels, "I will create a vicegerent (representative) on earth." They said, "Wilt Thou place therein one who will make mischief therein and shed blood; whilst we do celebrate Thy praises and glorify Thy holy name?" He said, "I know what ye know not." (Al-Baqarah, 2:30)

It is clear that Allah (swt) knew that human beings possessed the potential for violence. However, it appears that He also appreciated additional superior qualities unknown to the angels. Also, it is clear that Allah (swt) at the time did not choose to reveal those qualities to the angels.

Al-Qur'an also contains a discussion concerning the devil and his nature. The devil is considered part of the *jinn-kind*. Jinn-kind are a separate creation. Jinn are comparable to humans in the sense that they have free-will and will face a Day of Judgement. The devil's proper name is Iblis. Iblis is not considered a fallen angel. The name Iblis implies arrogance in defiance to Allah (swt). Al-Qur'an addresses this issue as follows:

> And behold, We said to the angles, "Bow down to Adam." And, they bowed down. Not so Iblis, he refused and was haughty. He was of those who reject faith. (Al-Baqarah, 2:34)

Iblis is also known as Shaytan. He is referred to as Shaytan when he is *the deceiver of mankind*.

> It should be borne in mind that Iblis and Satan (Arabic: Shaitaan) refers to one and the same being. The word Iblis is used when the Evil one's evil is limited to himself, and Satan when his evil affects others besides himself; or Iblis is the proud one, and Satan from (the word) "shatama," means "he became distant or remote". (Ali, 1995, Note 57)

Similar to the story in Beresit, there is a bountiful garden with a forbidden tree that should not be touched:

> And We said, "Oh Adam, dwell thou and thy wife in the Garden and eat of the bountiful things therein as (where and when) ye will. But approach not this tree, or ye run into harm and transgression." (Al-Baqarah, 2:35)

Iblis seduced Adam and his mate, and they rebelled against Allah's command. Accordingly, they fell from their state of *divine grace*. Nevertheless. Allah (swt) promised to send guidance to them to help them once again attain His favor:

> We said, "Get ye down all from here. And if, as is sure, there comes to you Guidance from Me, whoever follows My guidance, on them shall be no fear, nor shall they grieve. But those who reject Faith and belie Our signs, they shall be companions of the fire. They shall abide therein." (Al-Baqarah, 2:38)

Muslims believe that Al-Qur'an is the final revelation and guidance from Allah (swt). Iblis/Shaytan is the open enemy of humankind. And, guidance for forgiveness is obtainable within Al-Qur'an. The qadar of Allah (swt) fixes our overall destiny. Notwithstanding, we will be judged in part by and how we apply our free-will, and the resultant actions. The predestination aspects of the qadar may be challenging for clinicians to appreciate. Some Muslims may present with severe anxiety or complicated grieving issues. It is possible that these issues may be based on shame and guilt from a feeling of helplessness related to the individual's concept of predestination. It may be useful to explore the meaning of the *qadar of Allah*; especially with substance abuse and mental health patients/clients.

Comparative Discussions on the Psyche/Soul (Nafs)

From an Islamic perspective, the soul (nafs) is common to all human beings. Therefore, when Al-Qur'an discusses the topic, it may relate to more than just Muslims. Its principles may be universal. Indeed, certain specific verses (iyat) in Al-Qur'an address mankind (an-nas) as a whole. Others, specifically address the believers (al-muuminuun).

It is therefore reasonable that as human understanding in philosophy, psychology, and science develops, we will see, and be able to reflect upon the wisdom of revealed books, including Al-Qur'an. The challenge in finding this wisdom includes removing human narcissism/narcissistic traits, and permitting Divine wisdom to guide us. It may be useful to explore the works of several giants in the field of psychology as they relate to the psyche/soul (nafs). Psychologists often unintentionally mirror Islamic principles, or adequately explain Muslim behaviors. A comparison of their work to Al-Qur'an may be instructive.

Al-Qur'an

Humans have a soul (nafs) received as a gift from Allah (swt). It gives rise to the senses and other states of consciousness.

> He who created all things in the best way and He began the creation of man from Clay, and made progeny from the quintessence of a despised fluid. But He fashioned him in due proportion, and breathed into him of His spirit. And, He gave you (the facilities of) hearing and sight and understanding; little thanks do you give! (As-Sajda, 32:7-9)

Sigmund Freud

The soul/psyche is the part of the mind that is conscious. Consciousness give rise to our senses. Dr. Freud further elaborated and suggested that there were various levels of being including the *unconscious* and a *preconscious*.

> Now let us call "conscience" the conception which is present in our consciousness and which we are aware, and let this be the only meaning of the term "conscious." As for latent conceptions, if we have any reason to suppose that they exist in the mind-as we had in the case of memory-let them be denoted by the term "unconscious." Thus an unconscious conception is one of which we are not aware, but the existence of which we are nevertheless ready to admit on account of other proofs or signs (Freud, 1997, p. 49-50)

Alfred Adler

Dr. Adler also discussed the soul (an-nafs) and its relationship to consciousness. He made reference to *comfort* and *peace of mind* similar to the concept of *nafs al-Mutma'inna*, i.e. the satisfied/resolved soul.

> The human psyche has the capability of controlling consciousness. That is, it can make conscious something that our psyche wants brought to the surface, and conversely it can allow something to remain in the unconscious or even relegate it from the conscious to the unconscious, when the individual's comfort and peace of mind necessitate it. (Adler, 1998, p. 84)

Viktor Frankl

Dr. Frankl, the last of the famous three Viennese psychiatrists, suggested that the psyche and its ability to feel and think are essential to our humanness. Consistent with Qur'anic principles and, in my opinion, more than any other psychologist of his time, Dr. Frankl recognized the importance of addressing and labeling the spiritual side of mankind in clinical situations:

> Man lives in three dimensions: the somatic, the mental, and the spiritual. The spiritual dimension cannot be ignored, for it is what makes us human. To be concerned about the meaning of life is not necessarily a sign of neurosis. It may be, but then again, spiritual agony may have very little connection with a disease of the psyche. The proper diagnosis can be made by someone who can see the spiritual side of man. (Frankl, 1986, p. xvi)

Fitra

Al-Quran speaks on the nature of the soul (*an-nafs*). When the soul functions properly, it follows inherent guidance from Allah (swt). This is the *fitra*. The nature of the fitra is to be up-right (*haneefa*). Muslims consider Al-Islam (the submission to the will of Allah -swt) to be the religion of the *fitra*.

The Prophet Muhammad (pbuh) suggested that the fitra represented a purely human quality given the soul at birth by Allah (swt). In a conversation with several of his companions, he (pbuh) reported on a potential challenge between human nature (fitra) and its environment. In this case the family:

> ...Every child is born in the fitra and it is his parents who make him a Jew or a Christian... (Bewley, 2011, p. 90)

Al-Qur'an further states that adherence to the fitra is indeed the true and correct religion as follows:

> So set thy face truly to the religion being upright; the nature in which Allah has made mankind. No change (there is) in

> *[handwritten note: Could there be a reality that someone who doesn't believe in the soul work w/ Muslims?]*

the work (wrought) by Allah; that is the true religion; but most among mankind know not. (A-Rum, 30:30)

It may be that some fitra challenges experienced by the soul contribute to either well-being or to mental and emotional disorders. A negative fitra experience may result in some of the pathologies and disorders seen by clinicians. I identify indirect references to challenges of the fitra in the following works:

Dr. Sigmund Freud commented on a quality of *mental life* that appears to come with the human being at birth. He suggested that this *something* is evolutionary and part of *human archaic heritage*. I suggest that he indirectly made reference to the fitra:

> A new complication arises, however, when we become aware that there probably exists in the mental life of the individual not only what he has experienced himself, but also what he has brought with him at birth, fragments of phylogenetic origin, an archaic heritage. Then the question arises: in what does the inheritance consist, what does it contain, and what evidence of it is there? (Freud, 1939, p.125)

Dr. Carl Jung made similar observations about the fitra throughout his works. Most often it is implied in his discussions on archetypes. He suggested that the human mind developed in a similar process to the human body. While not mentioning the fitra by name, he suggested that this process was unconscious and a prehistoric quality given to humans:

> Just as the human body represents a whole museum of organs, each with a long evolutionary history behind it, so we should expect to find that the mind is organized in a similar way. It can no more be a product without history than is the body in which it exists. By "history" I do not mean the fact that the minds builds itself up by conscious reference to the past through language and other cultural traditions. I am

referring to the biological, prehistoric, and unconscious development of the mind in archaic man whose psyche is close to that of the animal. (Jung, 1968, p. 57)

It is possible that conflicts within the soul (pathologies and mental disorders) may be related to non-compliance to the nature of the fitra as offered in guidance given in Al-Qur'an and other religious sacred scriptures. Dr. Freud suggested, similar to Al-Qur'an, that certain social development helps to shape the fitra (instinct), as well as serve as a source of possible conflict. This conflict may lead to frustration, mental disorder, and antisocial behavior. When the soul is in proper alignment with the fitra it is at peace with itself and society:

> For the sake of uniform terminology, we will describe the fact that an instinct cannot be satisfied as a "frustration," the regulation by which this frustration is established are "prohibitions" and the condition which is produced by the prohibition as a "privation" ...We have found to our surprise that these privations are still operative and still form the kernel of hostility to civilization. (Freud, 1961, p. 12-13)

Dr. Jung similarly addressed the conflict between civilization, culture, and the fitra. He does not specifically mention religion. However, from my perspective, he mentioned a possible outcome when the soul (as a fitra instinct) is in conflict with a society or culture:

> What we call civilized consciousness has steadily separated itself from the basic instincts. But these instincts have not disappeared. They have merely lost their contact with our consciousness and are thus forced to assert themselves in an indirect fashion. This may be my means of physical symptoms in the case of a neurosis, or by mean of incidents of various kinds, like unaccountable moods, unexpected forgetfulness or mistakes in speech. (Jung, 1968, p. 72)

And finally, Dr. Victor Frankl weighs in on the discussion of the challenges between the fitra and instincts in relation to the lack of guidance and the susceptibility of the soul. Possibly drawing on his concentration camp experience, he suggested that without proper guidance people can be easily mislead to social oppression:

> Unlike an animal, man is not told by drives and instincts what he must do. And in contrast to man in former times, he is no longer told by traditions and values what he should do. Not, knowing neither what he must do nor what he should do, he sometimes does not even know what he basically wishes to do. Instead he wishes to do what other people do- which is conformism- or he does what other people wish him to do- which is totalitarianism. (Frankl, 2000, p. 94)

Dr. Frankl gives credence to a higher authority for the soul (an-nafs) by acknowledging that the drives and instincts of the soul cannot be its own source of inspiration:

> But just as drives and instincts cannot repress themselves, likewise the self cannot be responsible merely to itself. The self cannot be its own lawgiver. It can never issue any autonomous "categorical imperative" for a categorical imperative can receive its credential only from transcendence. (Frankl, 2000, p. 64)

Pastoral Care Models

Many pastoral care practitioners and pastoral counselors from various religious traditions are aware of and implement techniques for addressing the spiritual needs of their congregations or institutional charges. There are a number of definitions for pastoral care that can be used with Muslims. Dr. Howard Clinebell developed one that is particularly useful. He defined pastoral care as follows:

> Holistic pastoral care involves the use of religious resources for the purpose of empowering people, families, and

congregations to heal their brokenness and to grow toward wholeness in their lives. (Clinebell, 2011, p. 8)

The secular and scientific communities for the most part follow the medical/biological model. Dr. Viktor Frankl discussed what he called *medical ministry*. He suggested that similar to religious folks, medical people also minister to the sick. He further compared the therapeutic relationship between psychotherapy and religion:

> Medical ministry does not aspire to be a substitute for the proper cure of souls which is practiced by the minister or priest. What is the relationship between psychotherapy and religion? In my view, the answer is simple: the goal of psychotherapy is to heal the soul, to make it healthy; the aim of religion is something essentially different- to save the soul. (Frankl, 1986, p. xxi)

Dr. Frankl continued further by commenting on the possible psycho-spiritual benefits of religion and psychotherapy working together for holistic care as follows:

> But the side-effect of religion is an eminently psychohygienic one. Religion provides man with a spiritual anchor, with a feeling of security such as he can find nowhere else. But, to our surprise, psychotherapy can produce an analogous unintended side-effect. For although the psychotherapist is not concerned with helping his patient to achieve a capacity for faith, in certain felicitous cases the patient regains his capacity for faith. (Frankl, 1986, p. xxi)

I disagree with some aspects of Dr. Frankl's perspective. Islamically, the soul is within the preview of religion. Psychotherapy should concern itself with the domains of the mind and behavioral health. And, salvation comes from adherence to the guidance from Al-Qur'an and the ahadith. I believe that Dr. Frankl was guided in his discussion by a Judeo-Christian perspective of blood sacrifices for saving souls (salvation):

> For the bodies of those animals whose blood is brought into the holy place by the high priest as an offering for sin, are burned outside the camp. Therefore, Jesus also, that He might sanctify the people through His own blood, suffered outside the gate. (Hebrews, 13: 11-12)

Nevertheless, Dr. Frankl raises the possibility of an authentic working relationship between pastoral care practionners and psychotherapists. Together, they can treat the spiritual and emotional needs of the whole person.

In the Alcoholics, Anonymous and Narcotics Anonymous fellowships, there is a focus on the *higher power* for strength to overcome addictions. Certainly, Al-Islam considers Allah (swt) to be the higher power for curing spiritual diseases. Dr. Frankl mentioned the importance of achieving happiness. He suggested that, in part, happiness it is achieved by dedication to something greater than ourselves, a higher power:

> For success like happiness, cannot be pursued; it must ensue, and it only does so as the unintended side-effect of one's personal dedication to a cause greater than oneself or as the by-product of one's surrender to a person other than oneself. (Frankl, 1984, p. 17)

Training today for chaplains and medical students is steeped in the medical model. It is accepted in the remaining caregiving professions. This is especially true of mental health care. Dr. Jung also commented on the use of the medical model in psychiatry:

> All that is embraced today in the layman's idea of "psychoanalysis" originated in medical practice; and consequently most of it is medical psychology. It bears the unmistakable imprint of the physician's consulting-room, a fact which is evident not only in its terminology, but also in its framework of theory. (Jung, 1933, p, 30)

Dr. Jung further suggested that perhaps the physician had (and still has), too much influence on the field of psychology. While the medical model has its advantages, Dr. Jung suggested that the medical nomenclature may not be compatible with some approaches. I include pastoral care and chaplaincy in his discussion:

> We constantly come upon postulates which the physician has taken over from natural science, and in particular from biology. This fact has largely contributed to the hostility between psychology and the academic fields of philosophy, history and classical learning. Modern psychology is empirical and close to nature, while these studies are ground in the intellect. The distance between nature and minds, difficult to bridge at best, is increased by a medical and biological nomenclature which sometimes appears of practical utility, but more often severally taxes our good will. (Jung, 1933, p, 30)

Chaplains work in a variety of settings, i.e. hospitals, prisons, military, and nursing homes. Nevertheless, it seems that chaplains today are most noted for their work in hospitals. Indeed, it is the medical model that drives the education of chaplains. The founders of modern psychology were for the most part medical doctors/psychiatrist, i.e. Freud, Adler, and Frankl,

We are all in the business of caring for human beings in an effort to help them heal their bodies, minds, and spirits (souls). Clinicians may differ in theological perspectives and modalities. Nevertheless, the Muslim patient/client, like anyone in need, is interested in improved health and the best care possible. Meeting those objectives are the clinician's ultimately responsibility. Patients may be overwhelmed by the many different clinical practices available. They may be challenged to understand all the risks associated with various treatment and medications. They also can become bewildered by the onslaught of available, and sometimes questionable, information on the internet and in books. Dr. Jung addressed some of the challenges that the patient/client may have:

> Since the mind is common to mankind, it may seem to the

layman that there can be only one psychology, and he may therefore suppose the divergences between the schools to be either subjective quibbling, or else a commonplace disguise for the efforts of mediocrities who seek to exalt themselves upon a throne...The many-sidedness and variety of psychological opinions in our time is nothing less than astonishing, and it is confusing for the layman that no general survey of them can be made. (Jung, 1933, p. 28-29)

When Elephants Quarrel, the Grass Suffers

The giants of modern psychology were divided in their opinions on the value of religion in treatment. Some appear to value its importance. Others appeared ambivalent towards it, or dismissed it altogether. Dr. Sigmund Freud consistently, and especially in his later years, can be considered an opponent of religion. He dismissed religious ideas as wishful thinking and illusions:

> I think that we have prepared the way sufficiently for an answer to both these questions. It will be found if we turn our attention to the psychical origin of religious ideas. These, which are given out as teachings, are not precipitates of experience or end-results of thinking: they are illusions, fulfillments of the oldest, strongest, and most urgent wishes of mankind." (Freud, 1961, p. 38)

However, he was wise enough to acknowledge the limitations of his own speculations on religious doctrine. Nevertheless, he implied that science is the only basis for belief:

> Of the reality value of most of them we cannot judge; just as they cannot be proved, so they cannot be refuted. We still know too little to make a critical approach to them. The riddles of the universe reveal themselves only slowly to our investigation; there are many questions to which science today can give no answer...(B)ut scientific work is the only road which can lead to reality outside ourselves. (Freud, 1961, p.40)

Dr. Jung was candid in his reproach of both Drs. Freud and Adler for their positions on religion. He stated his concern as follows:

> Both schools (Freud and Adler), to my way of thinking, deserve reproach for overemphasizing the pathological aspects of life and for interpreting man too exclusively in the light of his defects. A convincing example of this in Freud's case is his inability to understand the religious experience, as is clearly shown in his book: The Future of an Illusion. For my part, I prefer to look at man in the light of what in him is healthy and sound, and to free the sick man from that point of view which colors every page Freud has written.... In any case, Freud's is not a psychology of the healthy mind. (Jung, 1933, p. 117)

In terms of the positive values in religion, and insight that can be gained by the clinician, Dr. Jung stated the following:

> As may be seen, I attribute a positive value to all religions. In their symbolism I recognize those figures which I have met with in the dreams and fantasies of my patients. In their moral teachings I see efforts that are the same as or similar to those made by my patients, when, guided by their own insights and inspirations, they seek the right way of dealing with the forces of inner life. (Jung, 1933, p. 119)

Dr. Viktor Frankl weighed into the discussion by acknowledging that psychotherapy and religion can work together in vicarious ways to address spiritual and emotional issues:

> Although religion may not aim at health, it might result in it. Psychotherapy, in turn, often results in an analogous by-product; while the doctor is not, and must not be, concerned with the patient to regain his belief in God, time and again this is just what occurs, untended and unexpected as it is. (Frankl, 1978, p.60)

Muslims see the religion of Al-Islam as more than a religion. It is a way-of-life. It is the standard by which we measure all things.

The eminent psychologists mentioned herein varied on their opinion concerning religion. When these giants and their disciples dispute among one another the patient may be left wanting. This condition is similar to the African proverb: *When elephants quarrel, the grass suffers.* Religious beliefs, when appropriate, can serve an area of exploration in counseling/treatment. It is my prayer that the foregoing discussion will add clarity and direction for caregivers to enhance their skills in order to provide the best treatment/counseling to Muslims and others.

Chapter 7: The Caregiver and Muslim Spiritual Assessment

A man said to the Prophet (peace and blessings of Allah be upon him), "Counsel me," so he (peace and blessings of Allah be upon him) said, "Do not become angry." The man repeated [his request for counsel] several times, and [each time] he (peace and blessings of Allah be upon him) said, "Do not become angry."

-An-Nawawi. Hadith No. 14

Holistic pastoral care involves the use of religious resources for the purpose of empowering people, families, and congregations to heal their brokenness and to grow toward wholeness in their lives

-Howard Clinebell, Basic Types of Pastoral Care, p. 8

Medical ministry does not aspire to be a substitute for the proper cure of souls which is practiced by the minister or priest. What is the relationship between psychotherapy and religion? ... In my view, the answer is simple: the goal of psychotherapy is to heal the soul, to make it healthy; the aim of religion is something essentially different- to save the soul. But the side-effect of religion is an eminently psychohygienic one...Religion provides man with a spiritual anchor, with a feeling of security such as he can find nowhere else. But, to our surprise, psychotherapy can produce an analogous unintended side-effect. For although the psychotherapist is not concerned with helping his patient to achieve a capacity for faith, in certain felicitous cases the patient regains his capacity for faith.

-Viktor Frankl, Doctor of the Soul, p. xxi

Pruyser's Diagnostic Variables

Given the preceding discussions, the question arises as to what would be a viable spiritual assessment model for a Muslim patient or client? Would it be different from assessments currently used? Are there particular criteria that should be included? Is there a religious context that must be captured? From my perspective, there are no necessary distinctions that have to be made. The human factors used in current spiritual assessment and mental health diagnosis also can apply to Muslims. However, very little of the pastoral care or psychology literature incorporates information or strategies specific to a Muslim perspective.

Paul Pruyser in his book *The Minister as Diagnostician* offers an appropriate and authentic clinical approach to spiritual assessments. His diagnostic variables can be used effectively with Muslim patients and clients by any caregiving professionals. His use of spiritual dimensions are compatible with Qur'anic principles. Pruyser's variables consist of:

- *Awareness of the Holy*: sense of those things that are sacred, revered, inspire awe or bliss, higher power, untouchable, or atheistic
- *Providence*: divine purpose/intervention, meaning of life, hope, issues of trust, afterlife, heaven/hell, fatalism
- *Faith*: religious tenets, rituals, beliefs, scripture, spirituality, humanism, magical thinking
- *Gratefulness*: ability to appreciate and value life, family, people, authentic humility, or lack thereof
- *Repentance:* responsibility for actions, regret, remorse, repairing harm, offense to G-d, understanding of penance, lack thereof
- *Communion*: relationship with mankind, family, society, church/ masjid/temple, peer groups, organizations; and
- *Vocation*: calling, willingness to participate with others, values interpersonal relationships, sense of mission. (Pruyser, 1963, 61-79)

Pruyser was emphatic that his diagnostic variables are only guidelines to help the pastoral clinician in his/her diagnostic interview. The categories are not meant to be casted in stone, but to focus the direction of the encounter.

Relationship of Pruyser's Variables to Al-Qur'an

The purpose of this section is to identify Qur'anic verses which may be used by the clinician to:

- Better understand Muslim spirituality
- Engage, explore, or evoke comments
- Explore meaning of spiritual distress
- Develop a strategy for assisting the patient/client
- Assist in movement towards improved spiritual wellness

There are numerous verses that can apply. I have selected to use three verses for each category. I believe that they will be most useful:

Awareness of the Holy:

To a Believer, only Allah (swt) is *Holy*. This attribute in Arabic is *Al-Quddus*. In the Alcohol Anonymous and Narcotic Anonymous fellowships submission to a higher power is important in the 12-step process. For Muslims, this higher power is Allah (swt). Willingness and readiness to submit to the higher power can be a first step to improved spiritual and mental health. The following verses may be used as a reference to explore issues of faith and belief:

> Allah is He, than Whom there is no other god; Who knows (all things) both secret and open; He, Most Gracious, Most Merciful. Allah is He, than Whom there is no other god; The Sovereign, The Holy One, The Source of Peace (and Perfection), The Guardian of Faith, The Preserver of Safety, The Exalted in Might, The Irresistible, The Justly Proud. (Al-Hashr, 59:23)

The earth, galaxies and universe are Allah's (swt) creation. Such a powerful Creator is capable of all things. He knows our every need. He is the source of all healing. Surrender to His magnificence and submission to His Grace are the path to wellness:

> It is He who made the sun to be a shining glory and the moon to be a light (of beauty) and measured out stages for it, that ye might know the number of years and the count (of time). Nowise did Allah create this but in truth and righteousness. (Thus) doth He explain His signs in detail, for those who know! (Yunus, 10:5)

Sometimes a Muslims may lose his way. He/She may feel that they have no purpose in life or may have forgotten, or lost their joy. Al-Qur'an informs us that Allah (swt) has a plan for each of us. We were not created for idle sport or for Allah's (swt) amusement. Remind the patient that life is sacred. This may alleviate a state of despair or depression:

> Not for (idle) sport did We create the heavens and the earth and all that is between! If it had been our wish to take (just) a pastime We should surely have taken it from those things nearest to Us, If We would do (such a thing). (Al-Anbiyaa, 21:16-17)

Possible Areas to Explore, Engage, Encourage, Evoke:

- Is there anything that the person holds to be sacred or untouchable? (e.g., Al-Islam, Allah (swt), Qur'an, life, or community)
- If so, how and to what extent does the person interact with the sacred? (e.g. intellectually, emotionally, or culturally)
- If not, explore those things which give life meaning or a sense of awe.

Listen and look for cues for further inquiry; however, allow the story from *the living human document* to unfold with little interference.

Providence:

This area explores the patient's appreciation of the *qadar* of Allah (swt) (Divine intention) towards the Believer. Here the clinician can discover the degree to which the person has a moral compass. Additionally, one can see how well the client is comfortable with his/her current life and/or projected future. Al-Qur'an offers guidance for the believers. This guidance describes the manner in which a person should live. It governs social interactions. It discusses earthly and heavenly rewards.

Bad luck is not an Islamic concept. Allah (swt) is in charge. Things happen according to the will of Allah (swt). Nevertheless, Muslims can be challenged by their unmet expectations. This condition may result in anxiety, depression or neurosis. There are several verses that may help clinicians and patients navigate these difficult spiritual waters:

> A.L.M. This is the Book. In it is guidance sure, without doubt, to those who fear Allah, who believe in the Unseen, are steadfast in (establish) Prayer, and spend out of what we have provided for them, and who believe in the Revelation sent to thee, and sent before thy time, and (in their hearts) have assurance of the Hereafter. They are on (true guidance) from their Lord, and it is these who will prosper. (Al-Baqarah, 2:1-5)

Al-Qur'an informs us that humans in part bring about their own troubles and challenging situations (perceived evil) that happens to them:

> Whatever good (Oh man!) happens to thee, is from Allah, but whatever evil happens to thee, is from thyself; and We have sent thee as a Messenger to (instruct) mankind, and enough is Allah for a witness. He who obeys the Messenger,

obeys Allah; but if any turn away, We have not sent thee to watch over them. (An-Nisaa, 4:79-80)

Everyone will be judged according to his/her action:

> Every man's fate We have fastened on his own neck. On the Day of Judgment, We shall bring out for him a scroll which he will see spread open. (It will be said to him) "Read thine (own) record; sufficient is thy soul this day to make out an account against thee." (Bani Isra'il, 17:13-14)

Possible Areas to Explore, Engage, Encourage, Evoke:

- Issues of trust
- Thoughts and feelings concerning the past, present, and/or future
- Fear of dying, The Hellfire, and the afterlife
- How does the person see his/her current situation in terms of Allah's (swt) will?
- Relationship with Imams, Islamic community acceptance of the individual, spiritual resources.

Faith

There is only one point faith. It is that there is only one G-d. Faith is the unique spiritual experience that occurs between the Creator and the creation. It is not rational. And, it evolves and locates itself in the spiritual heart. Faith is part of a conversation that takes place with the Divine. For some Muslims, feelings of faith can be experienced during prayer or in communion with others. Separation from prayer and community can bring about isolation and feelings of lost faith:

> It is He Who sent down Tranquility into the hearts of the believers, that they may add faith to their faith; for to Allah belongs the forces of the heavens and the earth; and Allah is Full of Knowledge and Wisdom; that He may admit the men and women who believe to gardens beneath which rivers flow, to dwell therein for aye, and remove their sins from

them, and that is in the sight of Allah the grand triumph. (Al-Fat-h, 48:4-5)

Al-Qur'an suggests that when a Muslim rejects Allah (swt), does not keep up prayers, and separates from the community, the result of such actions may be a loss of faith or submission to evil influences. When one makes these choices, the path to Allah (swt) is temporarily blocked. The *spiritual heart* may be kept from His mercy:

> As to those who reject faith, it is the same to them whether thou warn them or do not warn them; they will not believe. Allah hath set a seal on their hearts and on their hearing; and, on their eyes is a veil; great is the chastisement they incur. (Al-Baqarah, 2:6-7)

Belief is not just a personal phenomenon. It is related to specific actions. Muslims who neglect one or another of the components of belief may be affected negatively both spiritually and emotionally. They may feel that they are not living up to their religious obligations. They may feel the absence of Allah's (swt) Grace:

> The Believers, men and women, are protectors one of another. They enjoin what is just, and forbid what is evil. They observe regular prayers, pay Zakat, and obey Allah and His Messenger. On them will Allah pour His mercy; for Allah is Exalted in Power, Wise. (At-Tawba, 9:71)

Al-Qur'an informs the Muslim that Allah (swt) will not forgive a person who continuously rejects faith, believes, and rejects faith again. Such people increase in unbelief until they ultimately are lost.(An-Nisaa 4:137). This may be a concern for ambivalent American Muslims who succumb to societal pressures in order to assimilate. Especially, when they also feel that some aspects of American culture are decadent; yet, decadence is the norm, i.e. alcohol, licentious clothing and manners.

Possible Areas to Explore, Engage, Evoke:

- What role does faith play in the person's life?
- Quality of religious life
- What has worked, has not worked in the past for the person in terms of religious practice?
- Challenges and conflicts concerning faith or belief
- Religious satisfaction/dissatisfaction experienced

Gratefulness

In numerous places, Al-Qur'an admonishes humans not to be ungrateful. Allah (swt) gives life. He provides the bounties of the earth. He gives us spouses and children for comfort, and many more blessings. Many times our narcissistic ideations or behaviors cause us to forget our duty to Him. As a result, we may develop spiritual or mental disorders. To my mind, all sin is rooted in ingratitude. In certain respects, if we truly loved and appreciated the Lord, we would not willfully offend Him:

> It is He Who has spread out the earth for (His) creatures. Therein is fruit and date-palms, producing spathes (enclosing date). Also corn, with (its) leaves and stalk for fodder, and sweet-smelling plants. Then which of the favors of your Lord will you deny? (Ar-Rahman, 55:10-13)

We are dependent on Allah (swt) for our every need:

> There is no moving creature on earth but its sustenance dependeth on Allah. He knoweth its resting place, and its temporary deposit. All is in a Clear Record. (Hud, 11:6)

Help is available to those who ask and return to Allah's path:

> Then do ye remember Me; I will remember you. Be grateful to Me, and reject not faith. (Al-Baqarah, 2:152)

Possible Areas to Explore, Engage, Evoke:

- What role does Divine grace play in the person's life?
- How does the person understand religious duties?

- Areas of personal or religious disappointments
- Possible anger issues with Allah (swt)

Repentance

The Arabic word for repentance is *at-atauba*. In English it means *to return*. Al- Qur'an states that Allah (swt) may forgive all sins (inshallah) except associating partners with Him (An-Nisaa 4:48). The key to repentance is *the remembrance of Allah* (swt). This is called *dhikir Allah* (swt):

> Those who believe and whose hearts find satisfaction in the remembrance of Allah, for without doubt, in the remembrance of Allah do hearts find satisfaction; for those who believe and work righteousness is (every) blessedness, and a beautiful place of (final) return." (Ar-Ra'd, 13:28-29)

It is the practice in Al-Islam to confess *only* to Allah (swt). This is in part because the person may reveal a sin for which Allah (swt) has already forgiven them (Al-Misri, 2011, r35). Muslims are encouraged to cover the faults of their brothers and sisters for a similar reason. This behavior may be problematic for some counselors or certain medical personnel. It may take some time to develop a trusting therapeutic relationship with the caregiver. Additionally, confession can bring about a stigma that may affect marriage possibilities, or produce issues of shame and guilt.

Muslims are strict monotheists. It is forbidden to associate anyone or anyone thing with Allah (swt). He is unique and not in need of partner(s). He is separate and greater than His creation. The association of partner with Allah (swt) may be the *unforgivable sin* for a Muslim:

> Allah forgiveth not that partners should be set up with Him; but He forgiveth anything else, to whom He pleaseth; to set up partners with Allah is to devise a sin and heinous indeed. (An-Nisaa, 4:48)

Allah (swt) however is merciful and forgives sins, as He pleases; perhaps even for sincere penitents for associating partners with Him:

> He is the One that accepts repentance from His servants and forgives sins; and He knows all that ye do. And, He listens to those who believe and do deeds of righteousness, and gives them increase of His Bounty; but for the unbelievers there is a terrible Chastisement. (Ash-Shurah, 42:25-26)

The dimension of repentance may be the most difficult area for the clinician. The American culture is full of opportunities for youth and adults to engage in drinking, drugs, and promiscuous sex. While we know that some of these things go on within the Muslim community; still there is a great deal of denial both individually and collectively. It is important as well as sometimes challenging to maintain professional confidentiality (e.g. subpoenas of file records) and to build a trusting relationship with the client. The community is still very protective of the reputation of the Muslim family as well as its individual members.

Possible Areas to Explore, Engage, Evoke:

- Meaning of forgiveness to the person
- Emotional or societal impediments to forgiveness
- Readiness for change
- Explore meaning of divine punishment and hellfire/paradise
- Explore issues of possible isolation, depression, anger or rejection

Communion

Al-Islam is a family/community centered religion. The tradition builds upon the nuclear family, extended family (clan), Ummah (all other Muslims), and the nation (body politic). Individual prayers are required at least five times a day. Muslims may offer them alone or in congregation. The Friday congregational prayer, *Salaat-ul-Jummah* is obligatory on men. Much spiritual value is placed on saying any of the five daily prayers in congregation.

The American lifestyle is often not compatible with the prayer requirements. For example, when the various times for prayer arrive, a Muslim may be at work on a production line, in a business meeting, driving a bus, etc. where he/she cannot stop work to pray. Prayers must then be delayed. While this is permissible, delayed prayers are not recommended. This may be a challenge to a devout Muslim. There may be some residual resentment. Or, the person may use the American culture as an excuse for not fulfilling their religious obligations. Community and family are paramount. Al-Qur'an addresses this as follows:

> Oh ye who believe! fear Allah as He should be feared, and die not except in a state of Islam; and hold fast all together, by the rope which Allah (stretches out for you), and be not divided among yourselves; and remember with gratitude Allah's favor on you; for you were enemies and He joined your hearts in love, so that by His Grace, ye became brethren. And, ye were on the brink of the Pit of Fire, and He saved you from it. Thus doth Allah make His signs clear to you, that you may be guided. (Al-Imran, 3:102-103)

Al-Qur'an warns Muslims to protect one another from situations and people who may threaten there solidarity and religion:

> The Unbelievers are protectors, one of another; unless you do this (protect each other), there would be tumult and oppression on earth and great mischief. (Al-Anfal, 8:73)

Al-Qur'an suggests that humanity is of one creation. Allah (swt) sent messengers to every nation (people) to deliver His guidance. It is not for Muslims to judge societies or cultures. The truth of the books and prophets sent to various nations is enough. The challenge to Muslims is to follow their own guidance:

Mankind was one single nation. And Allah sent Messengers with glad tidings and warnings; and with them He sent the Book of Truth, to judge between people in matters wherein they differed. . . .(Al –Baqarah, 2:213)

Possible Areas to Explore, Engage, Evoke:

- Issues surrounding isolation from family or Ummah
- Social and cultural adjustment strategies
- Coping skill
- Anger issues
- Challenges to religious practices

Vocation

Vocation concerns itself with how well the Muslim puts all of the previous benchmarks together. This can be in a profession, participation in groups, mission in life, or volunteerism. The goal here is to explore and assess the spiritual wholeness of the person in the Muslim community, and the society in general.

In terms of the Muslim community itself, Al-Qur'an encourages Muslims to work together, be at peace with one another, and enjoin all to do good:

> Let there arise out of you a band of people inviting all that is good, enjoining what is right, and forbidding what is wrong; they are the ones to attain felicity. Be not like those who are divided amongst themselves and fall into disputations after receiving clear signs; for them is a dreadful chastisement (Al-Imran, 3:104-105)

At times Al-Qur'an addresses Muslims only (Oh you who believe). At other times it addresses all of humanity (Oh mankind). In terms of all humanity, Allah (swt) set trials and challenges for everyone. The best of us are the ones who excel in righteousness (Al-Hujurat, 49:13).

We are encouraged to compete with one another in the doing of good.

> To each is a goal to which Allah turns him; then strive together (as in a race) towards all that is good. Wherever ye are, Allah will bring you together; for Allah hath power over all things. (Al-Baqarah, 2:148)

All people must taste death, Muslim and non-Muslims alike. Additionally, we will all be judged according to our deeds. It does not matter what we think about one another our emotional or psychological challenges.

> Every soul shall have a taste of death, and only on the Day of Judgment shall you be paid your full recompense. Only he who is saved far from the Fire, and admitted to the Garden will have succeeded; for the life of this world is but goods and chattels of deception. (Al-Imran, 3:185)

Al-Qur'an encourages all humanity to work together for good. The best people ae the ones who are the best to each other. This implies that no individual or collective is innately better than another. When an individual presents with social anger issues, these verses may help to center the person. These verses may also be used to encourage tolerance and acceptance. This benchmark may help the client/patient to integrate their wellness tools.

Possible Areas to Explore, Engage, Evoke:

- Have you incorporated healthy religious values into your everyday relationships?
- What do you do that helps you find meaning in life?
- How have you shared this meaning with others?
- Do you have a responsibility to contribute to your community?

Selected Brief Case Studies

This section includes the summary of 5 brief cases. They represent actual encounters of several chaplains. The names have been changed to protect the confidentially of the patients. Three of the encounters took place in a hospital. The other two occurred in a more therapeutic counseling setting. Chaplain training usually teaches them to explore spiritual resources, feelings, and areas of meaning for the patient. For the most part, counselors work with the client to identify goals and objectives in a mutually agreed upon treatment plan. However, there are times when the clinician may need to combine both skills. Sometimes the reasons for this are cultural. This may be especially true when working with Muslims.

Muslim Immigrant women may present with male power differential issues. In certain cultures, women defer in relationships with their fathers, husbands, or employers. Subsequently, their inclination may be to passively defer to male clinicians. This may be one of the reasons to assign a female. Contrarily, certain females may feel that female clinicians are not as well qualified as male clinicians. Both these issues may complicate a client-centered therapeutic relationship. To further challenge caregiving, a woman may believe that Islamic traditions require that she may not be alone in a room with a male who is not her husband or a close relative.

Muslim men may present with similar or different challenges. Some males may be dismissive of the skills of female clinicians. They even may refuse to be treated by female personnel. At times in encounters, for confidentiality reasons, men may resist exploring their interactions or relationships with their family members. They perceive that line of inquiry as a threat to their authority or ego strengths. (Chaleby &Racy,1999)

Similar to the general population, Muslims may present with any number of caregiving needs. Some specific challenges follow:

> Islamic principles may be grouped under several headings. These include: spiritual and philosophical support and reassurance, guilt management, structuring of lifestyle, treatment of sexual dysfunction, behavioral management, correction of misconceptions about Islam, treatment of alcohol and drug abuse, and finally, folk healers-psychotherapists interchange. (Chaleby &Racy,1999, p. 156)

The following cases represent a chaplain's perspective. I use Paul

Pruyser's diagnostic variables as the model. I recommend this approach because it lends itself to a more effective spiritual assessment. The format for the brief case includes a description of the encounter, pastoral care concerns, intervention, and possible outcomes. When the caregiver determines that the patient needs a higher level of care, he/she should make an appropriate referral.

Case 1

Encounter

Safia is a 26-year-old Pakistani-born woman. She and her husband abide by strict Islamic traditions. She wears a hijab (head covering). Her arms are covered to her wrists, and her dress covers from her neck to her ankles. She and her husband received their graduate education in the US.

Safia is pregnant. She was on her way to Labor and Delivery at the hospital. This is her first child. Her husband dropped her off in front of the hospital. He then went to park the car. She stood on the curb waiting for him to return. While she waited, she felt the amniotic sac break (water broke). She panicked, and excitedly reported to the security guard standing nearby that *the baby is coming*!! The guard alerted the emergency staff. The staff went into crisis mode.

The husband panics when he does not see his wife on the curb waiting for him. Security staff takes him to her room. After much ado, Safia and her husband settled down in Labor and Delivery. The husband refused to leave her side. The husband insisted on speaking for his wife and directing staff on how to care for her. A female chaplain (ordained Baptist minister) happened to view the whole event and ministered to the family.

Case 1 Pastoral Care Concerns

- Patient's distress related to amniotic sac rupture
- Spiritual distress of the husband caused by not seeing his wife on the curb
- Feelings of being overwhelmed

- Fear of the unknown
- Feeling of shame related to being exposed to male medical staff during the emergency
- Hospital gown does not meet the religious standard for an appropriately dressed Muslim woman
- Patient may wish to keep her head covered (hijab)
- Unfamiliarity with the role of a chaplain
- Role, issues, and challenges of the husband (patriarchal issues

Case 1   Interventions

- Processed the patient's feelings and spiritual anxiety
- Consulted with medical staff on patient's desire to limit exposure to male personnel
- Advised medical staff on Islamic traditions of modesty, and the hijab
- Advised medical/staff on traditional role of Muslim men concerning the family matters
- Ministered to husband's spiritual distress, and feelings of mistrust
- Provided a pastoral presence for the family, medical staff, and hospital administration

Case 1 Outcomes

- Patient reported that she felt comfortable and respected
- Staff able to provide adequate and professional serves to patient
- Husband reported that he appreciated hospital's professionalism (customer satisfaction)
- Hospital developed a Muslim-friendly reputation

Case 1 Pruyser Diagnostic Variables

- Awareness of the Holy: Islamic Traditions Sacred and respected (hospital)
- Providence: Trust of staff and hospital procedures

(family)
- Faith: Spirituality and practices respected (family and hospital)
- Gratefulness: Appreciated how Muslim values were addressed (patient)

Case 2

Encounter

Ralph is a 52-year-old African American Muslim male. He has renal failure. He has been in kidney disease treatment (dialysis) for 7 years. He reports for treatment on Monday, Wednesday, and Friday. His daughter, a special needs child, died several years ago, as did his first wife. Patient presented with unresolved grief issues and related spiritual distress. Ralph reported that he fears that he will never survive a kidney transplant. He suggested that this fear is based upon his additional diagnosis of congestive heart failure (CHF).

Ralph stated that he chooses not wear traditional or identifiable Muslim attire. He stated that he kept his Christian name out of respect for his father. Nevertheless, he professes to be a devout Muslim. He reported loneliness related to alienation from communal life as a result of dialysis treatment 3 times a week. He reported that treatment does not allow him to attend Jummah Prayer on Friday afternoon. Ralph suggested that he is too tired after treatment to engage with other Muslims and non-Muslims friends and be sociable. He reported serious depressions related to the deaths of his daughter and wife. The chaplain make daily visit to the dialysis unit.

.Case 2 Pastoral Care Concerns

- Complicated unresolved grieving and spiritual distress related to death of wife and daughter
- Faith issues related to inability to attend required religious services or be in community with other Muslims

- Sense of patient's own mortality as a dialysis patient
- Finding meaning in suffering

Case 2 Interventions

- Actively listened to patient's story of suffering
- Helped patient process feelings related to death of wife and daughter
- Explored patient's meaning of suffering from an Islamic perspective
- Encouraged patient to explore possible spiritual resources
- Consulted with medical staff to assess whether patient's grieving rose to the level of a mental disorder

Case 2 Outcomes

- Patient had the opportunity to process aspects of his grief and spiritual distress
- Patient had opportunity to explore his feelings concerning his fear of death
- Patient had opportunity to grieve his loss of fellowship with Muslim community
- Spiritual connection established between Muslim and Christian chaplain

Case 2 Pruyser Variables

- Awareness of Holy: Islamic traditions sacred
- Providence: Meaning of life, fatalism
- Community: Islamic communal life
- Gratefulness: Appreciation for life, people, family
- Faith: Desire to practice religious obligations/rituals

Case 3

Encounter

Aisha is a 41-year-old African American female Sunni Muslim. She is married and has an eleven year old son. Her chart listed her condition as having Stage IV Bronchus/Lung Cancer. Doctors informed her that she had less than a month to live. Her husband and son often stay overnight in her room at the hospital. The husband insisted on being present during the chaplain visit. He expressed his displeasure with male staff visiting the room while his wife wears only a hospital gown. The husband insinuated himself into the chaplain's conversation with his wife. The wife appeared annoyed, yet deferred to her husband.

The patient described her feelings concerning various levels of pain she experienced. She wondered aloud whether her suffering would somehow benefit her in the afterlife. She stated that she did not want to die and leave her son without a mother. She reported that reciting Surah Al-Fatiha (opening chapter of Al-Qur'an) gave her much comfort. Aisha expressed concerns about being ritually impure for making prayers. She suggested that because she was confined to the bed, she did not have access to enough water necessary for making *wudu*. Aisha expressed anxiety concerning her remains. She feared that she would not have a proper Muslim burial. She reported that she and her husband did not affiliate with a particular community.

During a follow-up visit, the patient reported that her husband was in jail. She stated that he left the son alone at the shelter while he went to the laundry mat. The Agency for Children Services (ACS) took custody of the child.

Case 3 Pastoral Care Concerns

- Patient's fear of/preparation for death, and concern about the afterlife
- Inability to adequately discuss feels privately
- Hospital respect for Muslim religious traditions
- Husband's interference with best medical and spiritual care for patient
- Proper Muslim burial services
- Coordination with social worker

- Patient's spiritual stress related to uncertainty of future of husband and son

Case 3 Interventions

- Journeying and spiritually comforting patient during her end-stages of life
- Provided emotional space for patient to fully express her feelings and fears
- Pastoral presence to husband as he processed spiritual destress related to loss of his wife
- Pastoral presence as husband processed spiritual stress related to becoming a single parenthood
- Coordination with social worker on Muslim burial opportunities

Case 3 Outcomes

- Chaplain able to help patient process her immediate fears and concerns
- Patient reported that she felt better prepared for death
- Patient identified an appropriate and comfortable level of ritual purity for prayer given her restrictions
- Husband received useful burial information and assistance
- Husband and son better able to begin to address their grief
- Husband able to identify and accept a supportive role in his wife's end-stage process
- Hospital and healthcare team better able to provide effective and meaningful service to patient and family

Case 3 Pruyser Variables

- Awareness of Holy: Islamic traditions held sacred
- Providence: Meaning of life/death, afterlife
- Community: Family relationships; Islamic communal burial obligations respected
- Faith: Desire to practice religious obligations/purity rituals

Case 4

Encounter

Zubir is a 24-year-old Arab-American. He was born, raised, and college educated in Northern New Jersey. His family is wealthy. He lived a privilege life. The Bergen County Intoxicated Driver's Resource Center (IDRC) mandated Zubir to substance use disorder treatment for driving under the influence (DUI). This is his second offense. His license was suspended for 2 years. He spent over $2,000 in fines and 90 days in jail. A third offense carries a penalty of 10 years license suspension, 180 days in jail, as well as additional financial obligations.

Zubir started drinking heavily at age 15. He first used cocaine at age 21. His psychiatrist prescribed amphetamines (Adderall) for attention deficit hyperactivity disorder (ADHD), alprazolam (Xanax) a benzodiazepine for anxiety, and Percocet (opioid) for pain management for a back injury following a severe auto accident. Zubir reports a 5 years history and current recreational use of cocaine.

Patient is separated from his wife. He reported a legal custody battle concerning his 3 year old daughter. Patient reported fear at the thought of losing contact with his daughter. Patient reported being estranged from his family, due in part, to his substance use disorder. Patient stated that he experiences severe shame and guilt because he is *a drug-taking-Muslim*. Patient reported issues of loneliness and feelings of hypocrisy.

Case 4 Pastoral Care Concerns

- Patient willingness/ability to use faith (theology) and belief (praxis) as part of a recovery strategy from illicit drugs
- Patient's spiritual distress related to peer, family, and community pressures/rejection
- Patient's spiritual discomfort addressing mental health and illicit substances challenges (denial)
- Patient's guilt/shame related to challenges with his perceived religious obligations (especially prayer)

- Identifying spiritual resources
- Absence of a spiritual support network

Case 4 Interventions

- Spiritual assessment of readiness to change
- Consultation with psychiatrist
- Active listening
- Explore available options
- Reinforce spiritual strengths
- Recommend strategies for expanding support network
- Millati Isalmi (Muslim Recovery Program)

Case 4 Outcomes

- Patient identified next steps on the path to spiritual wellness
- Patient able to reduce self-hate-speak and focus on spiritual strengths
- Patient identified and committed himself to *action* in the stages-of-change model
- Patient able to make amends and begin to improve family relationships
- Patient stated he planned to initiated a study group for Muslim peers with substance use disorders

Case 4 Pruyser Variables

- Awareness of Holy: Surrender to Allah (swt) as the higher power
- Providence: Progressive improvement towards future without drugs
- Community: Reduced feelings of isolation, study group
- Gratefulness: Better able to appreciate life and family
- Repentance: Processed feels of spiritual distress related to guilt and shame for actions
- Vocation: Willing to participate in fellowship with others

Case 5

Encounter

Ramadhan is a 34 year old Afghani immigrant. He is married and lives with his wife and two children in New York City. Ramadhan reported that he worked as an armed security agent and English interpreter for an American company in Afghanistan. Ramadhan reported that he witnessed many atrocities. He stated that he saw innocent men, women, friends, and children shot or being blown to pieces. He reported *killing the bad guys.* Ramadhan reported that he is still plagued by visions and memories of all these events.

Ramadhan is in treatment for severe Post Traumatic Stress Disorder (PTSD), and moderate Major Depressive Disorder. His psychiatrist prescribed Ativan for anxiety, and Lexapro for the PTSD. Ramadhan stated that he immigrated to the US in part because of retaliation and threats against him and his family.

Ramadhan reported that he feels shame and guilt for the work he did. He stated that he has lost his faith. He stated that he feels that Allah (swt) will punish him for his actions. He reported that he feel rejected by and isolated from the Afghan community.

Case 5 Pastoral Care Concerns

- Apparent crisis of faith and belief
- Spiritual anxiety/fear for himself and family
- Spiritual/Religious meaning patient placed on taking a life
- Meaning of isolation from Afghan and/or Muslims community
- Techniques/Strategies for spiritual recovery, spiritual strength, and wellness
- Absence of a spiritual/communal support network

Case 5 Interventions

- Assess and explore patient's spiritual health/stremgth
- Help identify spiritual strengthening resources

- Actively listen to narrative on perceived religious conflicts
- Pastoral presence through narrative on the meaning of taking life
- Explore spiritual roots of fear, shame, and guilt
- Explore patient's opportunities for networking

Case 5 Outcomes

- Improved spiritual coping skills for processing shame and guilt
- Identification of Qur'anic spiritual resources
- Identification of support groups/persons
- Strategies for improving relationships with the Muslim community

Case 5 Pruyser Variables

- Awareness of Holy: Questioning nature and will of Allah (swt)
- Providence: Concern for the Hereafter and possible punishment
- Community: Reduced feelings of rejection and isolation, protecting family and community
- Gratefulness: Opportunity to immigrate to US; safety for self and family
- Repentance: Processed feels of spiritual distress related to guilt and shame for actions

The information included herein is brief and not an exhaustive analysis of the possible needs of Muslim patients and clients. Each caregiver will bring (inshallah) his/her own talents and professional understanding to each encounter. It is my prayer that this information will be useful (inshallah). Thank you in advance for your contribution to the spiritual wellbeing of Muslims

APPENDICES

A. Honorifics Used in This Book

Subhanau wa ta'ala – Glorified and Exalted is He (swt)
Sallallahou alayhe wasallam- Peace be unto him (pbuh)
'Alayhis-salam – Peace be upon him (as)
Radiya Allahu'anhu/a May Allah be pleased with hum/her (ra)

B. Transliterated Useful Phrases

Allahu'akbar - Allah (swt) is the Greatest
Alhamdulillah- Praise is due to Allah
As-salaamu 'alaikum- May peace be upon you
Astaghfirullah- I ask Allah's (swt) forgiveness
Azzawajal- Mighty and the Majestic is He
Barakallah- May Allah (swt) bless you
Bismillahir Rahmanir Raheem- In the Name of Allah(swt) The Gracious, The Merciful
Hasbulallah- May Allah (swt) suffice you
Id al-Adhha- Celebration after the Hajj
Id al-Fitra- Celebration after Ramadan
Inshallah- If it pleases Allah (swt)
Jazakallahkhaira- May Allah (swt) reward you with goodness
La ilaha ilallah -There is no god but Allah
La hawla wa laa quwwata illa Billaahi- There is no power or strength except with Allah (swt)
Mashallah- It is as Allah (swt) willed it to be
Pbuh- Peace be upon him (reference to Prophet Muhammad)
Subhan'Allah - Glory be to Allah
Swt- Glorified and Exalted is He
Nafs Al-Ammarah- The soul inclined to evil
Nafs Al-Lawammah- The self-accusing soul
Nafs Al-Muhamah- The understanding soul
Nafs Al-Mutma'inna- The soul inspired to piety
Nafs Al--Radiyah- The well-adjusted soul
Yarhanakallah - May Allah(swt) have mercy on you (when someone sneezes)

Walaikum as- salaam- And upon you be peace

C. Selected Arabic Words

Adab- Manners
Al-Islam- Submission to the will of Allah bringing peace
Al-Qur'an- Revelation given to the Prophet Muhammad (pbuh)
Asr- Ritual prayer in the mid-afternoon
Ayat- Sign, a verse of Al-Qur'an
Bida'- Innovation
Dhuhr- Ritual prayer just past noon
Dhikr- Prayer of remembrance of Allah (swt)
Farj- Ritual prayer at dawn (first light)
Fiqh- The understand of a particular school of Islamic thought
Hadith- Sayings and practices of the Prophet Muhammad (pbuh)
Hajj- The greater pilgrimage to Mecca required of adult Muslims
Halal- Permitted by Shari'a (Islamic law)
'Ibada- Act of worship
Iddat- Waiting period before a women can remarry after a divorce
Ijtihad – To exercise personal judgement in legal matters
Iman- Faith, actualized confidence in Allah (swt)
Imam- Religious leader of masjid, temporal leader of activity
Isha- Ritual late night prayer
Jihad- Challenge, struggle
Jummah- Ritual Friday noon congregational prayer
Ka'ba- Temple in Mecca build by the Prophet Ibrahim (as) and his son Prophet Isma'il (as)
Kafir- Unbeliever
Kutba- Sermon, delivered at the Jummah prayer
Maghrib- sunset prayer (dipped below the horizon)
Masjid- Place of prostration, usually a dedicated space
Muhmin- Believer
Qibla- Prayer direction towards the Ka'ba in Mecca
Ramadan- Sacred month of fasting
Ruh- The spirit
Salat- Ritual prayer consisting of fixed movements
Shahada - Profession of faith

Shirk- To associate anything as a partner of Allah (swt)
Sunnah- Traditional practices of the Prophet Muhammad(pbuh)
Surah- Chapter of Al-Qur'an
Tafsir- Explanation of the meaning of Al-Qur'an; exegesis
Tawhid- Oneness of Allah
Tawba- Returning to correction action, repentance
Umrah- nonmandatory lesser pilgrimage (hajj)
Wudu- Ritual washing in preparation for prayer

REFERENCES

Abdul-Wahhab, Muhammad bin (1996) *Kitab at-tauhid*. Riyad, Saudi Arabia: Dar-us-Salam Publications.

Abu Abd al-Rahman, Ahmad (al-Nasa'i), (1930). Cairo, Egypt: Misriyya Press vol. 6, pg.11. In Abdur-Rahman, Rauf (1995). *The Islamic view of women and the family*, 3rd. ed. Alexandria, VA: Al-Saadawi Publication.

Al-Misri, Ahmad (n.d.). *Reliance of the traveler*. Nuh Ha Min Keller (Ed.) (2011). Beltsville, MD: Amana Publications.

Association for Clinical Pastoral Education (ACPE). Information for prospective students https:// www.acpe. edu/ACPE/ _Students/FAQ _S.aspx retrieved June 14, 2016.

Association for Clinical Pastoral Education (ACPE) *Standards & manuals*, 2010 Processing Complaints of Ethics Code Violations in ACPE, Preface, Addendum April 2014, http://s531162813.onlinehome.us/pdf/2010%20Manuals/ 2010% 20 Ethics%20 Manual.pdf, retrieved 12/12/14

Adler. Alfred, (1998). *Understanding human nature (*trans. C. Bret). Center City, Minnesota: Hazelden.

Ahmad, Zain-Din (1994). *Summarized sahih al-Bukjari*. Trans. Muhammad Khan. Ryihad, Saudi Arabia: Makraba Dar –us- Salam.

Akbar, Na'im (2004). *The evolution of human psychology for African Americans*. In Black psychology (4th ed.). Hampton, VA.: Cobb & Henry Publishers.

Al-Albaani, Muhammad Nasir (no year given). *The Prophet's prayer*, translated bin Hasan, Usama. New Delhi, India: Al-

Haneef Publications, Millat Book Centre.

Alexander, Curtis. E (1981), *Elijah Muhammad on African American education*, Chesapeake, Virginia: ECA Associates.

Ali, Abdul-Latif (2003). *The admiral family circle Islamic community (Doctoral Project)*. South Bend, IN: Graduate Theological Foundation.

Al-Jibaly, Muhammad (2003). *Sickness regulations & exhortations*, 2nd ed. Arlington, Texas: Al-Kitaab &As-Sunnah Publishing

Ali, Muhammad (1974). *The Muslim prayer book, 4th ed.*.Lahore, Pakistan: Ahmadiyyah Anjuman Isha'at Islam

Ali, Muhammad (1995). *The Holy Qur'an*. Lahore, Pakistan: Ahmadiiyyah Anjuman Isha'at Islam, Inc.

Ali, Osman (2005). The imam's role in meeting the counseling needs of Muslim communities in the United States. In *Psychiatric Services*, Vol. 56, No. 2, pp. 202.

American Bible Society (1980). *The Holy Bible*, King James Version, New York. NY.

American Medical Association (AMA) Code of Medical Ethics, http://www.ama-assn.org/ama/pub/physician-esources/medical-ethics/code-medical-ethics/principles-medical-ethics. Retrieved 12/12/14.

American Muslim Council (1992). *The Muslim population in the United States (*1st ed.). Washington, DC.

American Psychiatric Association (2013). *Diagnostic and statistical manual of mental disorders* (5th ed.). Arlington. VA.

American Society of Addiction Medicine (ASAM) (2013). *The ASAM criteria: Treatment criteria for addictive, substance-related and co-occurring conditions*, 3rd ed, Carson City, NV: The Change Companies.

An-Nawawi, Abu Zakaria (n.d.). *Forty hadith*. E. Ibrahim & D. Johnson-Davies Trans. (1997). Chicago, IL: Independent Publisher's Group.

Association for of Clinical Pastoral Education (ACPE). *Information for prospective students.* Retrieved March 25, 2013 from https//www.acpe.edu/faq.htm.

Associated Press (AP) (2006).*Subject 1: DD5s referencing 10/11/06 plane crash into building at 524 E. 72nd Street* Intelligence Division Intelligence Analysis Unit, October 16, 2006, retrieved July18,2014.http://hosted.ap.org/specials/interactives/ documents/nypdnypd/ planecrash.pdf.

Barker, Kenneth (1985). *The new international version study Bible*. Grand-Rapids, Michigan: Zondervan Publishing House.

Bewley, Aisha Abdurrahman (2011). *Al-Muwatta of imam Malik ibn Anas,* Inverness, Scotland: Madihan Press.

Belviranli, Ali Kemal (1983). *The principles of Islam*. Konys, Turkey: Sebat Offset Printers.

Boisen, Anton (1936). *The living human document. I*n Robert Dykstra, (Ed.) (2005). *Images of pastoral care.* Danvers, MA: Chalice Press.

Breggin, Peter (1991). *Toxic psychiatry*. New York, NY: St. Martin Press.

Brenner, Daniel (2002) et. al. *Embracing life and facing death*. New

York, NY: CLAL-The National Jewish Center for Learning and Leadership.

Bynum, Bruce (2012). *The African unconscious: roots of ancient mysticism and modern psychology*. New York, NY: Cosimo Book.

Chaleby, K. & Racy, John (1999). *Psychotherapy with the Arab patient* (Eds .). Shawn McLaughlin/QSOV

Counsel of American Islamic Relations (CAIR) (2013). *Legislating fear: Islamophobia and its impact in the US*, Washington, DC.

Cartwright, Samuel A, (1851). Report on the diseases and physical peculiarities of the Negro race. *The New Orleans medical and surgical journal*. Retrieved July 11, 2014 from http://www.balderexlibris.com/index.php?post/The-New-Orleans-medical-and-surgical-journal.

Clark, Kenneth & Clark, Mamie (1959). Emotional factors in racial identification and reference in Negro children. *Journal of negro education*. Washington, DC: Howard University.

Clinebell, Howard (2011). *Basic types of pastoral care & counseling* (3rd Ed.). Nashville, TN: Abington Press.

College of Pastoral Supervision and Psychotherapy (CPSP) *Code of professional ethics*, Section 1100, http://www.pastoralreport.com/ The_Standards_of_CPSP_2014.pdf, retrieved 12/12/14

Cuomo, Andrew (2011). New York State executive order. 26https://www.governor.ny.gov/news/no-26-statewide-language-access-policy. Retrieved June 6, 2014.

Counsel of American Islamic Relations (CAIR) (2010). *Two men accused in subway imam (African American) attack hit with hate crime charges.* Legislating fear: Islamophobia and its impact in the US, Report 2013 and NY Daily News, December 9, 2010.

Cushmeer, Bernard (1971). *This is the one, messenger Elijah Muhammad.* Phoenix, AZ: Truth Publication,

DeGruy, Joy (2006). *Post traumatic slave syndrome: American's legacy of enduring injury and healing,* Portland, OR: Uptone Press.

Diop, Cheikh Anta (1991). *Civilization or barbarism.* Chicago, IL: Lawrence Hill Books,

Doi, Abdur Rahman (1984), *Shariah: the Islamic law.* London, England: Ta-Ha Publishers Ltd.

Federal Bureau of Investigation, (1942). *Moorish science temple of America*, File no. 100-4094. Retrieved June 6, 2013 20https:// vault.fbi.gov/Moorish%20Science%20Temple% 20of%20America.

Esack, Farid (1997). *Qur'an liberation & pluralism.* Oxford, England: One World Publications.

Everly, George, Jr., and Dewey, Rob (2002) et al. *Pastoral crisis intervention.* Ellicott City, MD: The International Critical Incident Stress Foundation, Inc.

Everly, George, Jr., and Mitchell, Jeffrey T (2002). *Critical incident stress management: advance group crisis intervention a workbook*, 2nd Edition (revised), Ellicott City, MD: The International Critical Incident Stress Foundation, Inc.

Fadl, Khaled (2008). The ugly modern and the modern ugly. In Omid Safi (Ed.) *Progressive Muslims: On justice, gender, and pluralism* (p.33). Oxford, England: One world Publications

Faizi, S.F. (1997). *Sermons of the prophet.* New Delhi: Kirab Bhavan,

Federal Bureau of Investigation (1942). Moorish science temple of America, File no. 100-4094. November 2, 1942 https://vault.fbi.gov/ Moorish%20 Science%2 0Temple% 20of%20 America. Retrieved June 8, 2008.

The Final Call (2014). Volume 33, No. 15. Chicago, IL:FCN Publication.

Frank, Viktor (2000). *Man's search for ultimate meaning.* New York, NY; Basic Books.

Frankl, Viktor (1988). *The will to meaning.* New York, NY: Meridian Book, Penguin Group.

Frankl, Viktor (1986). *Doctor and the soul.* New York, NY: Random House.

Frankl, Viktor (1984). *Man's search for meaning.* New York, NY: Pocket Books.

Frankl, Viktor (1979). Psychotherapy and essentialism: Selected papers on logotherapy. In William Gould (1993). *Frankl: Life with meaning.* Pacific Grove, CA: Brooks/Cole Publishing Company.

Freud, Sigmund (1997). *General psychological theory,* New York. NY: Simon & Schuster. (Original 1911)

Freud, Sigmund (1961). *The Future of an Illusion (J.* Strachey, Ed.). New York, NY: W.W. Norton & Company.

Freud, Sigmund (1959*). Group psychology and the analysis of the ego*. New York, NY: Norton & Company. (Original 1922)

Freud, Sigmund (1939). *Moses and monotheism* (trans .K. Jones,). New York: Vintage Book.

Gershon, Michael D. (1998). *The second brain*. New York, NY: HarperCollins Publishers.

Graber, Ann V. (2004). *Viktor Frankl's logotherapy*, 2nd ed, Lima, OH: Wyndham Hall Press.

Gould, William (1993). *Frankl: life with meaning*. Pacific Grove, CA: Brooks/Cole Publishing Company.

Guraya, Muhammad Yusuf (1996). Origins of Islamic jurisprudence (2nd. Ed.). Lahore, Pakistan: Sh. Muhammad Ashraf Publishers.

Habib, Samar (Ed.) (2010). Islam and homosexuality (vols.1&2). Santa Barbara, CA: Praeger ABC- CLIO.

Hasan, Masudul (1995). *History of Islam*, vols. 1&2, revised edition. New Delhi, India: Adam Publishers and Distributors.

Health and Human Services (HHS) (2001). *National standards on culturally and linguistically appropriate services (CLAS) in health Care.* Office of Minority Heath, Washington, DC.

Hossein, Imran N (1997). *The caliphate-the hejaz and the Saudi-wahhabi nation-state*. Kuala Lumpar, Malaysia: Ummavision Sdn, Bhd.

Huntington, Samuel P. (1997). *The clash of civilizations and the remaking of world order*. New York, NY: Simon & Schuster.

Ibrahim, I.A. (1991) (ed.). *A brief illustrated guide to understanding Islam*. Houston, TX: Darussalam Publishers.

Ihsan Bagby (2001) et al, *The mosque in America: a national portrait*, in American religious identification survey 2001, The Graduate Center (CUNY).

Isenberg, Nancy (2016), *White trash, the 400-year untold history of class in America*. New York, NY: Viking/Penguin Random House.

Jackson, Vanessa (n.d.). In our own voice: African-American stories of oppression, survival and recovery in the mental health systems. Vernellia R. Randall (2008) (e.d.) Retrieved June 5, 2008 from http://academic.udayton. edu/health/01status/metnal01.htm.

The Joint Commission (2010). Advancing effective communication, cultural competence, and patient- and family-centered care: A roadmap for hospitals. Oakbrook Terrace, IL.

Jung, C.G. (1968) (Ed.). *Man and his symbols*. New York, NY: Dell Publishing.

Jung, C.G (1933). *Modern man in search of a soul*. New York. NY: Harcourt, Inc.

Kepel, Gilles (1997). *Allah in the west,* Stanford California: Stanford University Press.

Khan, Qamaruddin (1982), *Political concepts in the Quran*. Lahore, Pakistan: Islamic Book Foundation

Kly, Y. N., (1989), *The anti-social contract*. Atlanta, GA: Clarity Press Inc.

Kly, Y .N. (1990). *International law and the black minority in the U.S.* (3rd ed,). Atlanta, GA: Clarity Press, Inc.

Kobeisy, Ahmed Nezar (2004). *Counseling American Muslims*, Westport, CT: Praeger Publishers.

Kornfeld, Margaret (2000). *Cultivating wholeness*. New York, NY: The Continuum International Publishing Group, Inc.

Kramer, Max (2013). Sexual orientation: The ideological underpinnings of the gay advance in Muslims majority societies as witnessed in online chat rooms. In Samar Habib (Ed*.). Islam and homosexuality* (p.134) (Vol.1*).* Santa Barbara, CA: Praeger ABC-CLIO.

Kugle, Scott (2013). *Homosexuality in Islam*: Critical reflection on gay, lesbian, and transgender Muslims. London: Oneworld Publications.

Kunjufu, Jawanza (1985). *Countering the conspiracy to destroy black boys*. Chicago, IL: African American Images.

Le Bon, Gustave (2002). *The crowd: A study of the popular mind.* Mineola, NY: Dover Publication.

Learner, Rokelle (2009). *The object of my affection is in my reflection*. Deerfield Beach, FL: Health Communications, Inc.

The Lost-Found Nation of Islam (NOI) (1994). *Petition for U.N. assistance under resolution 1503.* Atlanta, GA.

Mahdi, As-Sayyid Isa (1989). *The book of laam (*2nd ed.). Brooklyn, NY: The Original Tents of Kedar.

Maslow, Abraham (2011). *Toward a psychology of being.* Mansfield Centre, CT: Martino Publishing.

Ministry of Hajj and Endowments-MHE (AH 1411/1990). *Holy Qur-an*. Al-Madinah, Saudi Arabia: King Fahd Holy Qur-an Printing Complex.

Muhammad, Amir Nashid Ali (2001). *Muslims in America*, (2nd. ed,). Beltsville, MD: Amana Publications.

Muhammad, Elijah (1965). *Message to the black man in America.* Chicago: Muhammad's Temple No.2,.

Muhammad, Warithuddin (1982). *Prayer and al-Islam*, Chicago. IL: Muhammad Islamic Foundation.

The Nation of Islam (NOI) 2014). *The final call*. Volume 33, No. 15, Chicago: IL: FCN Publication.

New York Daily News (NYDN) (December 9, 2010). *Two men accused in subway imam (African American) attack hit with hate crime charges.*

New York State. *Executive order 26. statewide language access policy*. October 6, 2011

New York Times, (May 4, 1993). Citing Dawud Assad of the Muslim World League in NYC.

Nomani, Manzoor (n. d.). *Islamic faith & practice*. Karachi, Pakistan; Shakeel Printing Press.

Nu'man, Fareed (1992), *The Muslim population in The United States.* Washington, D.C.: American Muslim Council.

Pedersen, Darlene (2005). *Psych notes*. Philadelphia, PA: F. A. Davis Company.

Poussaint, Alvin (1972). *Why blacks kill blacks*. New York, NY: Emerson Hall Publishers.

Poussaint, Alvin (1974). Building a strong self-Image in Black children. In *Developing positive self-images and discipline in black children*, Jawanza Kunjufu, Chicago, IL: African American Images.

Pruyser, Paul W (1976). *The minister as diagnostician*. Philadelphia. PA: Westminster Press.

Ricoeur, Paul (1970). *Freud and philosophy: An essay on interpretation*. New Haven, CT: Yale University Press.

Rogers, Carl R. (1995). *On becoming a person*. New York, NY: Houghton Mifflin Company.

Shad, Abdur-Rahman (1978). *Duties of an imam* A. H. Siddiqui (Ed.). Chicago, IL: Kazi Publications.

Shakespeare, William. Julius Caesar, Act 2, Scene 2. In *The Yale Shakespeare* (1919). New Haven: Yale Press,

Stack, Liam (up-dated February 15, 2016). *American Muslims under attack*. New York Times. http://www.nytimes,com /interactive/2015/1 2/22/us/ Crimes-Against-Muslim-Americans.htm, Retrieved July 16, 2016

Taymiyyah, Ahmad ibn Abdul-Halim ibn (2010). *Diseases of the hearts and their cures* (trans. by S. Amrad). Birmingham. Great Britain: Dar as-Sunah Publishers (5th ed.).

The Joint Commission (2010): *Advancing effective communication, cultural competence, and patient- and family-centered care: A roadmap for hospitals*. Oakbrook Terrace, IL.

Thanawi, Ashdaf Ali (Ed.) (n.d). *Khutubat-i-jumau'ah,* No. 7. Lahore, Pakistan: Sh. Muhammad Ashraf, Publishers.

Nation of The Final Call , FCN Publication, Chicago, Ill., Volume 33, No. 15, 2014

Trotter, Wilfred (1921), *Instincts of the herd in peace and war.* Great Britain: Filiqurian Publishing, A.363132.

U.S. Congress. Pub. L. 88-352, title VI, Sec. 601, *Civil rights act of 1964* , July 2, 1964, 78 Stat. 252.

U.S. Department of Health and Human Services (2000). Administration on Developmental Disabilities. Curricula Enhancement Module. http://www.ncccurricula.info/culturalcompetencehtnl. Retrieved June 12, 2016.

U.S. Department of Health and Human Services (2001). Office of Minority Heath. *National standards on culturally and linguistically appropriate services (CLAS) in health care.* Washington, DC.

UN Department of Public Information (1998). Preamble. *Universal declaration of human rights (*DPI/876-40911 Rev. 1993.)

UN General Assembly (2006). *The convention on the rights of persons with disabilities.* resolution A/RES/61/106.

US Supreme Court (1856). *Dred Scott v. Sandford.* 60 U.S. 393

Volf, Miroslav (2011). *Allah: A Christian response.* New York, NY: HarperCollins Publishers.

Washington, Harriet (2006). *Medical apartheid: The dark history of medical examination on black Americans from colonial times to present*, New York, NY: Doubleday.

Webster's New World Dictionary (1966). New York, NY: The World Publishing Company. College ed.

Welsing, Frances Cress (1991). *The Isis papers the key to the colors*. Chicago, IL: Third World Press.

Williams, Walter L. (2010). Islam and the politics of homophobia: The persecution of homosexuals in Islamic Malaysia compared to secular China. In Samar Habib (Ed.). *Islam and homosexuality* (Vol.1). Santa Barbara, CA: Praeger ABC-CLIO.

Yazid, ibn Muhammad (ibn Majah) (1953). *Sunan*. In Abdur-Rahaman, Rauf (1995). *The Islamic view of women and the family (*3rd. ed) (p.17). Alexandria, VA: Al-Saadawi Publication,

Zeno, Muhammad bin Jamil (1996). *The pillars of Islam & iman.* Riyahd, Saudi Arabia: Dar-us-Salam Publications.

AUTHOR BIOGRAPHY

MUHAMMAD HATIM, Ph.D, D.Min., is a respected religious leader, human rights activist, educator, lecturer, and counselor. He retired as an Imam with the Admiral Family Circle Islamic Community (Admiral Family) in New York City after 18 years. He was a longtime student of Shaykh Dr. Abdullah Latif Ali. He directed the Admiral Family Justice Ministry (prisons/courts). As the Admiral Family's Non-Governmental /United Nations (NGO/UN) Representative, he participated in the United Nations religious and human rights activities both here in the US as well as Geneva, Switzerland. Dr. Hatim volunteered as a Red Cross Disaster Chaplain after the World Trade Center tragedy in NYC. He is the *Imam Warith Deen Muhammad Professor of African American Muslim Studies* at the Graduate Theological Foundation in Indiana; Board Certified Clinical Chaplain (BCCC) and Pastoral Counselor (BCPC) by College of Pastoral Supervision and Psychotherapists (CPSP); and both a Certified Drug and Alcohol Counselor (CADC) and Certified Co-Occurring Disorder Professional (CODP) in New Jersey. Early in his career, Dr. Hatim held positions as a Civil Engineer, Environmental Protection Specialist, and Acting Director of Civil Rights with the US Environmental Protection Agency (EPA), Region 2, NYC; Managed a transit company, and was the Director of the Office of Transportation on St Croix and Acting Director of the Office of Transportation (territorial) for the US Virgin Islands. Dr. Hatim completed a 4 year apprentice and worked as a journeyman Tool and Die Maker for the General Electric Company in Philadelphia, Penna. He is currently a Board Member of Opera Ebony (NYC).